MIRACLES IN BETWEEN

Grace Reaches Down.
Faith Reaches Up.

JIM COPENHAVER

XULON ELITE

Xulon Press Elite
2301 Lucien Way #415
Maitland, FL 32751
407.339.4217
www.xulonpress.com

© 2022 by Jim Copenhaver

Paperback ISBN-13: 978-1-6628-5454-5
Ebook ISBN-13: 978-1-6628-5455-2

Dedication

To my mom and my brother
who never got to read this book.
I love you both and miss you both.
Your faith has become sight.

What Are Others Saying About
Miracles In Between?

"Miracles In Between… Grace reaches down, faith
reaches up. In one simple title, Jim Copenhaver has
encapsulated the story of God's interaction with us,
and our interaction with Him. You will be blessed, as
you read this book, to discover the miraculous ways
that God works in our lives. Jim has provided in clear
language what it means to put our faith into action and
reminds us that God truly can do the supernatural. I
believe your faith will be strengthened as you read this
book, because I know the author believes in the truth
of his words. May the Lord use this work for His glory!"

—Wendell Brown
Founder – Tragedy Into Triumph
District Superintendent – North Central Ohio
District Church of the Nazarene

"I have known Jimmy since he was a young child. His love for the Lord is greatly seen in his daily walk. I truly believe that the Lord has greatly used him in the writing of this book, "Miracles in Between." He vividly shows the workings of God's grace and faith in the life of a believer. This book shares the importance of God's Word in the life of every child of God. This book is an easy read and I highly recommend it."

—Pastor Dan Wingate Pastor Emeritus
West Hill Baptist Church Wooster, Ohio

"We all have seasons in our lives when we need a miracle. In his new book, Miracles In Between: Grace Reaches Down, Faith Reaches Up. Pastor Jim Copenhaver has given us an encouraging, faith-building handbook for dynamic Christian living. Read it, believe it and practice it and watch what God will do!"

—Dr. Dave Earley
Associate Professor of Pastoral Leadership
and Evangelism, Liberty University

"Jim Copenhaver is a dynamic and energetic evangelical pastor, and spiritual leader for many Christian groups. Here he has brought the wisdom and focus of his 20 years of pastoral ministry to guide the skeptical reader to accepting God's offer of eternal salvation and grace through Jesus Christ. To the believer, Pastor Jim leads the way to growing his/her faith into a life of walking daily in the love and power of the Lord."

—Wallace W. White
Retired Pastor, and Author

"The combination and connection of grace and faith, a topic sorely needed for the unsaved and greatly desired by Christians wanting to go deeper in their walk with Jesus."

—Mark Miller
Former NFL Quarterback
Board Chair Of Hall Of Fame Area FCA
Canton, Ohio

"It is God which works in us both to will and to do His good pleasure..." This double infinitive in Philippians 2:13 describes the simple two-step process of how God intervenes in our lives. The book "Miracles In Between" is a personification of Philippians 2:13 in the family of Jim, Angela and Hutson Copenhaver. While working in the orchards of Ohio, a totally new world of stepping out on faith alone began the as Jim acknowledged, that God was calling him to start a Church. From that moment forward, the book describes this process as God reaching down in Grace and this family reaching up in faith. What has been happening in between "grace reaching down and faith reaching up" is how the title "Miracles In Between," was discovered. This book doesn't dodge the highly personal questions and struggles of this challenging faith journey from singing in the orchards of Ohio to the pastorate of a Nazarene Church. Jim, thanks for allowing me the privilege of witnessing God at work in your life."

—Dr. Norm Pratt
Retired Pastor, and Evangelist

"If you know Pastor Jim, you know his energy is going lift you (and push you) from page one of this book. If you don't know Pastor Jim, you will hear his heart-beat in these pages – a heart beating for his Lord and Savior, Jesus Christ. Grab on to this book. Hold on tight! And, enjoy the ride!"

—Mark Zimmerman
Mornings with Mark & Gabe
Heartfelt Radio | 91.9fm | Barberton, OH

"I have come to know and respect Jim Copenhaver for his sincere humility and authenticity. Whether personally or corporately, Jim's goal is not to impress people; but rather to connect with them and point them to Jesus. That characteristic can be seen through this book. Jim uses his unique gift of simplifying the Gospel into bite-size pieces and arranges them into easily digestible concepts. He bridges the gap between grace and faith in a practical way that makes sense to those who are Christians and those who are still making their faith journey. May God use this book to open your eyes and strengthen your faith."

—Dr. Gary Colboch
Senior Pastor
Grace Church, Pompano Beach, FL

Foreword

And when He had looked around at them all, He
said to the man, "Stretch out your hand." And
his hand was restored as whole as the other.
(Luke 6:10)

Have you ever needed encouragement? I know
I have. There are times in all of our lives when
we just need to hear hopeful words...words that lift
us up...words that enlarge our faith.

In his book, Miracles In Between: Grace Reaches
Down. Faith Reaches Up, Jim Copenhaver provides
words of HOPE! Through his retelling of familiar
passages from the Bible, you will not only find new
insights and perspectives, but food for your soul. His
delightful style of writing touches the heart, as well
as the mind.

Put this book on your night stand, on your desk,
or in your car. Pick it up and read a chapter here
and another chapter there. Or, if you desire, read

it through in one sitting. It will remind you of God's grace which reaches down to you daily. And, it will encourage you to reach up in faith.

—Gary L. McIntosh, Speaker and Writer

Introduction

❦

This book is all about God's grace and our faith. It's a reflection of some of the things that I have learned and experienced through the combination of God's grace, my faith, and God's Word. I am so thankful for the amazing grace of God. I am so thankful for the power that exists in faith; when grace and faith collide, miracles happen!

When Grace And Faith Collide, Miracles Happen

I guess *collide* isn't the best word to use, it sounds a little violent. Let's try a different word. How about *collude?* Ugh! No. That sounds even worse, how about, *combine?* That's it, when grace and faith combine, miracles happen in between.

I remember my first trip to Union Station in Washington DC. I was amazed at the vast expanse of train tracks I saw as I gazed down through a foggy, overlooking, catwalk window. Each track pointed in a different direction, yet they all combined, they were still connected. All the trains on their separate tracks were running perfectly, without any collisions with any of the other trains going in different directions and eventually all of the tracks leaving the station merged into one track headed in one direction. On an even greater spiritual scale, God's grace and our faith work together. Which happens first? Which one triggers the other? How can they work together, holiness and sin, spirit and flesh? Interesting topics to explore, and I am not sure I understand this great mystery, but I know one thing: when God's grace combines with human faith, miracles happen.

This is a deep, deep, theological discussion, but don't worry. I have had the privilege of discussing these topics in classrooms and over cups of coffee with many great minds, some professors, and some theologians. I have done the hard work, so you can just read my book and enjoy it. I am certain at times this book will challenge your thinking. But as you read, I want to encourage you to lay aside your denominational background and approach this book with an open heart, mind, and soul.

I really have never considered myself to have a great mind—and I hated school—so the fact that I have written a book is a miracle in itself! I have never really desired to have a great mind, just a great faith in God, and that's exactly why I wrote this book, to let the world know what happens when we believe that with God all things are possible.

I love simplicity. No matter what the topic or the subject of discussion, I work hard to make it as simple as I possibly can. When I preach, I do my best to leave my listeners with a sermon that they could put into one sentence, no matter how short or long I preached or how well or poorly I preached. When I consider the relationship between God's grace and people's faith, there's no doubt it is a very complex topic for our minds to grasp. The topics of salvation, redemption, and grace are really complicated matters but God has made them simple enough for even a child to understand it. His glory, and His grace can all be found in the simplicity of life.

His Glory And His Grace Can Be Found In The Simplicity Of Life

I love fishing in local rivers, ponds, or in the depths off the Florida Gulf Shores. I enjoy having conversations with friends over a meal even if the meal isn't very good. It's fun to put the windows down and drive in the summer nights while seeing the moonlight reflect off my truck. There is beauty in simplicity.

Plato considered the beauty found in simplicity when he wrote, "Beauty of style and harmony and grace and good rhythm depend on simplicity—I mean the true simplicity of a rightly and nobly ordered mind and character, not that other simplicity which is only a euphemism for folly." Understanding grace and faith all begins with an understanding of the truth of God's Word.

In his book, *What The Faith Is All About,* Dr. Elmer Towns says this about the importance of God's Word, "If we want faith, we must begin with a correct under-standing of the Word of God. The more we know of the Bible, the more faith we can have, and the more correctly we know the Bible, the more effec-tive our faith."

With that thought in mind, let's look at a passage from God's Word found in Ephesians 2,

But God, who is rich in mercy, because of His great love with which He loved us, even when we were dead in trespasses, made us alive together with Christ (by grace you have been saved), and raised us up together, and made us sit together in the heavenly places in Christ Jesus, that in the ages to come He might show the exceeding riches of His grace in His kindness toward us in Christ Jesus. For by grace you have been saved through faith, and that not of yourselves; it is the gift of God, not of works, lest anyone should boast. For we are His workmanship, created in Christ Jesus for good works, which God prepared beforehand that we should walk in them. (Ephesians 2:4–10)

I have heard many great sermons preached from this passage of Scripture and I have heard many great discussions and debates on this passage, but they have always left me searching for more and more. It seems I hear an accurate definition of God's grace until I hear an even better definition of it. The same is true with faith. It seems I hear an accurate definition of faith until I hear another great definition of it.

Merriam-Webster defines *grace* as, "unmerited divine assistance given to humans for their regeneration or sanctification." That's pretty good. Merriam-Webster defines *faith* as, "belief and trust in and loyalty to God." But if I would ask you to define grace and faith, I would assume your answers would be a little different.

Perhaps you would respond quickly with a biblical definition of faith and refer to Hebrews 11, which says, "Now faith is the substance of things hoped for, the evidence of things not seen" (Heb. 11:1).

But to find a biblical definition of God's grace, good luck! It is not found in Scripture. Unmerited favor? Yes. A prayer before a meal? Yes; okay, maybe not.

Favor or approval? Absolutely! So how could something that is so important, and so amazing, not be clearly defined in the Bible? I believe it's because grace is God's responsibility, and no matter how hard we try we will never truly or fully understand His grace, and that is really okay.

Isaiah 55 explains why, where it says, "'For My thoughts are not your thoughts, Nor are your ways My ways,' says the Lord. 'For as the heavens are higher than the earth, So are My ways higher than your ways, And My thoughts than your thoughts'" (Isa. 55:8–9).

Grace is God's responsibility. Grace is His job. Saving grace belongs to Him. God's grace is in full out pursuit of our faith and faith is our job. Faith is our responsibility. Faith is up to us. Whether we believe or we don't is completely up to you and me.

Grace Is God's Job; Faith Is Our Job

God doesn't need our faith, but we can't receive His grace until we have faith in Him. We can see it, we can sense it, we can hear about it, we can even know about it, but we can't receive it in our lives until we believe, until we have faith in Him.

God has given His Word as a means of grace to us and not only does it contain the words of eternal life, but it is also binds Him to keep His promises to all mankind, which is a really good thing for you and me.

When we are trying to define grace, we are trying to explain the very essence and existence of the eternal God and that is exactly what the Bible does from Genesis to Revelation and everywhere in between. The Bible is a letter of grace written by God Himself. What will we do with it: Will we believe it? Will we allow His Word to change us? The Bible was given to us that we could be complete and equipped for every good work. God inspired men through His Holy Spirit to write the many books of the Bible. Without this inspiration we'd have just another book, but with it, we have the Word of God. In God's Word, we see God's grace is on full display, covering all of time and all of mankind, and because of that, we really have no excuse to miss out on the grace of God.

God has made Himself evident to all of us through His Word, His Spirit, His gospel, and through all of His creation. Romans 1 describes that truth to us this way, "For since the creation of the world His invisible attributes are clearly seen, being understood by the things that are made, even His eternal power and Godhead, so that they are without excuse" (Rom. 1:20).

We must not have a ho-hum attitude about the Word of God, we must believe it, live it, preach it, and teach it. The Word of God makes possible the faith to receive the promises of God through Jesus Christ our Lord. In John 5, Jesus says: "Most assuredly, I say to you, he who hears My word and believes in Him who sent Me has everlasting life, and shall not come into judgment, but has passed from death into life" (John 5:24).

His Word, received by faith, produces the greatest miracle since the birth of Jesus Christ! It was God who wrapped up The Word in flesh and delivered the good news of salvation to all the world—grace, faith, and miracles in between—let's go!

1

It's a Boy!

And the Word became flesh and dwelt among us,
and we beheld His glory, the glory as of the only
begotten of the Father, full of grace and truth.
(John 1:14)

Now in the sixth month the angel Gabriel was sent by God to a city of Galilee named Nazareth, to a virgin betrothed to a man whose name was Joseph, of the house of David. The virgin's name was Mary. And having come in, the angel said to her, "Rejoice, highly favored one, the Lord is with you; blessed are you among women!"

But when she saw him, she was troubled at his saying, and considered what manner of greeting this was. Then the angel said to her, "Do not be afraid, Mary, for you have found favor with God. And behold, you will conceive in your womb and bring forth a Son, and shall call His name JESUS. He will be great, and will be called the Son of the Highest; and the Lord God will give Him the throne of His father David. And He will reign over the house of Jacob forever, and of His kingdom there will be no end."

> Then Mary said to the angel, "How can this be, since I do not know a man?"
>
> And the angel answered and said to her, "The Holy Spirit will come upon you, and the power of the Highest will overshadow you; therefore, also, that Holy One who is to be born will be called the Son of God." (Luke 1:26–35)

I know. I know. You're probably thinking about a low budget Jesus film, complete with dangling microphones, atrocious long straggly hair, shaggy beards, and phony British accents. Or possibly something even worse...a children's church drama production! Now, there is a terrifying thought; especially if you were forced to be in one as a child, like I was!

I guess I have turned out okay. Anyway, back to the main scene. For a moment, I want you to lay aside all of the Christmas traditions, good or bad, and focus on these words spoken to Mary because the journey of God in the flesh all starts here, with a divine dialog between the virgin Mary and Gabriel, an angel of the Lord. Let's break it down.

"Hey, Mary, you're going to have a baby. Congratulations! It's a boy!"

But wait there's more: "He is the Son of God! The Savior! The Messiah! The Redeemer!"

Those words spoken by Gabriel demand quite a response. Now, there is no doubt Mary had been acing her ancient Hebrew Health classes, because she fires back with a brilliant question. She politely asks, "How can this be, seeing I haven't had sexual relations with a man?"

Think of all the thoughts running through the mind of Mary at this moment: How can this be? How will my parents react? This is Cray-Cray! There's no chance! I didn't have sex. I'm going to be grounded for life. It goes against all the laws of nature. It is absolutely absurd...It's...it's impossible! Yes, that's it! It. Is. Impossible. Impossible! That's what she'll go with.

So Mary continues the conversation, "I am sorry. That is impossible." She must feel certain that this response will end the conversation. After all, impossibilities are the end for mankind.

Impossibilities, however, are where God does His greatest works. So then comes one of the most powerful statements of all time. It contains the answers to all theological debates. It's a statement that all of Scripture tethers on.

Impossibilities Is Where God Does His Greatest Works

Gabriel says to Mary, "For with God nothing will be impossible" (Luke 1:37 NKJV). Look at those seven words. Just for a moment really look at those words. Please don't rush by them.

For with God Nothing Will Be Impossible.

The New Century Version translates the verse, *"God can do anything!"* (Luke 1:37 NCV).

Wow, God can do anything! There is absolutely no limit to His power! There are no boundaries He can't overcome! He never has to get approval. He never has to consult with His financial committee. He never needs a majority vote. God can do anything!

From an extremely young age, Mary had been trained and taught in the characteristics and works of Jehovah-God. She had been taught over and over again lessons like:

Jehovah-Jireh—God provides. (Genesis 22)
Jehovah-Rapha—God heals. (Exodus 15:22–26)
Jehovah-Nissi—God wins. (Exodus 17:8–15)
Jehovah-Shalom—God of peace (Judges 6:24)
Jehovah-Raah—God is our shepherd (Psalm 23:1)
Jehovah Tsidkenu—God of righteousness (Jeremiah 23:6)
Jehovah-Shammah—God is here (Ezekiel 48:35)

She had been taught that God is all-powerful. She had been taught that He is all-knowing. She had been taught that God is everywhere and that God is eternal.

But being taught about God is one thing. Theologians call that "theology." But an individual person taking God at His word is totally different, that's called "faith."

Many teach, preach, and live theology, but it seems few teach, preach, and live what I'll call "me-ology," by which I mean the knowledge and belief that God loves me, God speaks to me, God works in me, God has plans for me, and with Him no detail of me is overlooked because He knows things about me that I don't even know about myself.

In this moment, when Gabriel brought His message to Mary, God became real in Mary's life and, better yet, God became personal in Mary's life. You see, Mary had heard that God had delivered Noah and his family from the flood. She had heard that God had delivered the children of Israel from the chains of Egypt. She believed all those stories she had heard from her childhood, but all of those things had happened to others not to her personally.

Mary had heard about the promise of the coming Messiah but she never dreamed she would have anything to do with it. She knew that God moved in mysterious and miraculous ways, but for God to do so in her life was highly unlikely! She knew His work had been recorded in the ancient texts, but He had been silent for so long. So, how could this be? In an instant, locked in time, and recorded in God's Word to all of us as readers now, the Virgin Mary is suddenly challenged to believe that God can do anything. This statement is ringing in her ears. We can imagine Mary's thoughts: *Can it really be true? Can God really do anything? Anything?*

As you read this book, I want you to think about this statement: God can do anything. I want you to pretend for a moment that statement was said directly to you, because even though all of our circumstances may be different, how we respond to that living statement from God's active Word says everything about our spirituality and our personal connection with God. All of life stems from this statement proclaimed to Mary by an angel of the Lord.

Many times we panic and try to do things on our own. Maybe we just don't believe that God can do all things. Maybe we don't care. Maybe we're too independent to ask. Maybe we simply disobey His word. Maybe we're looking in all the wrong places.

But know this: The God of the Bible is the God who can do anything.

Because of her faith in God's Word, Mary yielded her will. Because of her faith in God's way, Mary yielded her life. Because of her faith in God's grace, Mary yielded her heart, mind, body, and soul to the word of God that had been spoken to her. She responded with a bold proclamation in Luke chapter 1, "Behold the maidservant of the Lord! Let it be to me according to your word" (Like 1:38). In modern English, Mary said: "God, whatever you want to do in my life, do it. I'm Yours."

Think about it, there are many ways Mary could have reacted. There are many ways she could have responded. She could have said, "I need a couple days to think about this . . .." I mean it is the Son of God, the Messiah, the Savior of the world the angel is telling her about! Who could fault her for a response like that?

She could have said, "Would it be okay if I texted a friend about this? I need some input from a friend." Who could fault her for wanting to consult with a friend?

She could have said, "Hey, Gabe, can I check my schedule? I'll let you know?"

Everyone is busy, right?

Social media is pretty popular, maybe she could have posted a poll to see what her followers thought?

Like us, Mary had tons of excuses. Remember, we're talking about being the mother of Jesus Christ, the Son of God, the Messiah that she had heard about, learned about, and hoped and prayed would come soon to save her people. The one who would take away the sins of the world. She had every right to respond however she wanted to.

The same is true with us. Don't we all have a choice to believe or not believe? Don't you? In all reality, we all have the right to respond to the Word of God any way we want. When God's grace invades our life, we are faced with a choice. Theologians calls this "free will." God has freed our will to choose Him or not, to trust His Word or not, to obey Him or not.

So, who could really blame Mary on how she would respond to this unbelievable news?

But when she heard the fact that God can do anything, she believed and responded with, "Let it be done according to Your Word." We should respond the same way when God speaks to our hearts. In that moment, Mary made a choice to put her faith into action. She chose to display her faith to all the world. She chose to leave no doubt that she believed God could and can do anything! And then in a flash, Gabriel left, and the conversation was over. Just as quickly as it began, it was done. But the story had really just begun. Grace reached down. Faith reached up. Because of Mary's faith, we can be blessed. Because of Mary's faith, we can experience the grace of God through His Son, Jesus Christ.

Every time I read this passage of Scripture, I wonder how many times God speaks to my heart and I respond with fear or unbelief or my own personal non-negotiables. How about you? I know you and I have never been asked to birth the son of God, but I am certain that God is speaking something to our hearts right now, no matter where we are in life. No matter if we are young or not so young, God is speaking to us through His Word, through His Holy Spirit, through His gospel, through all of His creation. How are we responding?

Are we responding with faith or are we responding with hesitation?

Are we responding with faith or are we responding with questions?

Are we responding with faith or are we responding with excuses?

One of the greatest mistakes we make as humans is that we have a tendency to put a question mark where God has put a period. God can do anything. Period.

God wants to do miraculous things in your life, and He can. God can do anything!

He wants to make a faith transaction with you and it all hinges on your response to that statement: God can do anything. It is vital that we remember that, even though completing certain tasks may be beyond possible for us, we are not working toward them alone. God makes the impossible possible every single day. Impossibilities are where God does His greatest work.

Do you believe?

2

Anything?

When Jesus heard it, He marveled, and said to those who followed, "Assuredly, I say to you, I have not found such great faith, not even in Israel!" (Matthew 8:10)

S ince the conversation between Gabriel and Mary and the immaculate conception took place, many throughout history have denied the virgin birth of Jesus Christ.

Let me say this again: Mary was told that she was going to birth the Son of God before she had sexual relations with any man. Mary was a virgin. Many have downplayed it and acted like it's not that big of a deal, but I would strongly argue, it is a big deal! It's a really big deal. In fact, it's a make it or break it deal breaker!

I have discussed this topic with many educated men and women, who declare it would be a scientific impossibility for a virgin to give birth to a child, and guess what? They are 100 percent correct! Please disagree with anyone who tells you that I don't like science! I respect the efforts of scientists and admire their area of work. I would hope they would say the same about my efforts in my area of work; however, what many misunderstand is that scientific impossibilities are not a challenge for God.

Science does a wonderful job describing how life happens, but science comes up short explaining why life happens. What happens in between the *how* and the *why* of life is where faith comes in. The Bible makes it clear that we are to "walk by faith, not by sight" (2 Cor. 5:7).

We are to walk by faith, not by sight. We must stop believing everything that we see going on around us and start paying attention to what is going on inside of us. We must live our lives based on what God's Word says not on what we see.

We walk by faith by trusting God. Faith in God makes the impossible possible! This is where God can really show up and really show off. This is where miracles happen. I truly believe our faith moves God in big ways.

Our Faith Moves God In Big Ways

Our impossibilities give Him the opportunity to show to all the world that He is God and there is nothing impossible for Him. Mary, who was a virgin, conceived by the power of the Holy Spirit of God and gave birth to the Son of God and His name is Jesus. There has never been anyone born like Jesus before Him and there will never be anyone born like Jesus after Him.

A virgin conceived, a virgin gave birth, the impossible took place. Jesus was, and is, a legit one of a kind. He was made a little lower than the angels. He was given a human body. He was flawless. He was perfect. He was sinless. Jesus came to pay the price for eternal life for all of us. Jesus took on human flesh from His mother, the Virgin Mary, but Jesus received His bloodline from God.

Jesus died in human flesh, but Jesus defeated death, hell, and the grave because of His divine nature. Jesus finished the work that His heavenly Father sent Him to do. He took on human finite life to give us all infinite life.

You see, there has never been a person in all of history who has made a greater impact on the world than Jesus Christ. His teachings are etched in all of time and they continue to resonate in our hearts and souls after more than two thousand years. We have seen many great people come and go and along with them, their words, their ideas, their legacies have gone with them.

You need an example, right? I'll give you a simple one. Without cheating: Can you name the twenty-third President of the United States?

Final Jeopardy song playing in your ear...

Not Cleveland, not Adams, not McKinley...It was Benjamin Harrison. Harrison was the twenty-third President of the United States, serving from 1889 to 1893. He was one of the first politicians to ever campaign from his front porch. There, he would deliver short speeches to delegates who would visit his home in Indianapolis. He and his administration led an extensive economic legislation, which included the McKinley Tariff, which imposed monumental protective trade rates and the Sherman Antitrust Act. He also led the charge on the creation of the National Forest Reserves through an amendment to *The Forest Reserve Act of 1891*. This was all big stuff—cultural shaping works—a significant President of the United States of America; yet, for the most part, Harrison has been forgotten in the files of history, and he is not alone.

Many men and women of significance have and will be forgotten along with their social and global impact, but not Jesus Christ. His life, awe, wonder, words, and legacy live on and on! Christ's life and His teachings continue to shape our world. He is still a controversial public figure, and He hasn't posted, tweeted, given a speech, or made an appearance in over 2000 years.

Many still despise Him; many still adore Him. Millions gather on a weekly basis to study His words, to cry out to Him in prayer, to worship Him with their hands lifted in praise—some in caves, some in cathedrals—but all share the same driving force to draw closer to Him. In fact, as time goes on, He seems to be more relevant in the lives of those who follow Him. His truth seems to be even more needed in our social, political, and scientific debates. His teachings and words seem even more significant in our lives as individuals as we navigate through the uncertainties of this life. I guess that is why the great apostle Paul describes Him this way, "And He is before all things, and in Him all things consist" (Col. 1:17).

Jesus continues to make significant impacts on our churches, society, and our ideologies. He is the beginning and the end; we are the in-between. There can be no denying this: A choice must be made when we think about Jesus Christ, either choose to believe He is who the Bible says He is or choose to not believe.

While on earth, every step Jesus took and every miracle He performed left His followers and critics astonished. For some, all they could do was worship Him and adore Him. They couldn't get close enough to His presence. They would hang on the edge of their seats to be certain they wouldn't miss a word He spoke. They wanted more of the life that Jesus was proclaiming and offering. Yet, strangely enough, for all the multitudes that adored Him, there were just as many that hated Him. They seemed to question everything He said. They despised His teachings and His miracles, and eventually their disdain was so intense they killed Him with seemingly no remorse.

How could Jesus be loved by so many and hated by so many all at the same time? That question still demands an answer today. Many people right now would lay down their lives for Jesus Christ, and many would curse His name and despise Him, His followers, and His church! Contained in the Bible we find four gospels of Jesus Christ. These are books that give an in-depth look at the words and ways of Jesus Christ as He walked and talked with His disciples and the world. These four gospels were inspired by the Holy Spirit and written by ordinary men named Matthew, Mark, Luke, and John. These men were called, they were chosen, to be disciples of Jesus as He lived on earth. Through their writings, we know them as His apostles.

In their books, we find around thirty-seven miracles of Jesus Christ recorded for all to read. However, the books leave a miracle loophole on the exact amount of miracles Jesus performed while He was on the Earth, they were just off the charts.

John writes in, chapter 21, "And there are also many other things that Jesus did, which if they were written one by one, I suppose that even the world itself could not contain the books that would be written. Amen" (John 21:25). I have often wondered what miracles Jesus did that weren't recorded? Were they even greater than what we have recorded? Was it all just too much for us to handle?

I can't wait to have dinner with Matthew, Mark, Luke, and John in heaven. Maybe at Jonah's Calabash, McDavid's, or even Peter's Hash & Ham, and ask them what those miracles were. I would love to hear all about them. Eternity won't be long enough to discuss them all! In each of the accounts, the apostles make it clear to all their readers that Jesus was and is a world changer! In fact, I don't think world changer is a great enough description for Jesus; in all reality He is an everything changer!

From the moment the Angel Gabriel announced that He would be born, and Mary said, "Yes!" The world changed forever! The world received a gift like nothing it had ever received before. Life would never be the same; not only for His mother Mary, but for all of mankind! This includes you and me. Every single one of us is now faced with a decision to believe or not to believe in Jesus Christ; to respond with a "yes" or to respond with a "no."

Do you know what the first miracle performed by Jesus was? Let me give you a hint. It happened at a wedding? There was a shortage of a party supply? You got it. He could turn water into wine. I don't know about you, but I struggle making macaroni and cheese; but Jesus turned water into wine!

No Extra Ingredients Are Needed When Jesus Is In The Kitchen

Jesus took water and transformed it into wine! He took a common item and turned it into a delicacy. He took a life essential and made it the life of the party! He was showing the world that if we would crave life-giving water that He was offering, we'd be satisfied in ways we could never dream of or imagine. No extra ingredients are needed when Jesus is in the kitchen!

Can you imagine the money wineries could make off of this if they were able to harness that power today? Anyway, that's another book, I'll let another pastor write that one. Maybe a Baptist pastor! Kidding! I'm only kidding. What a start!

The miracles didn't stop there. The Bible tells of people being healed instantly—totally healed—from treacherous conditions. We're not talking about the Sunday morning sniffles that keep some from church, we're talking about some extreme medical conditions! Jesus healed those with diseases that doctors and medical experts could offer those in need no solutions or hope for, but when Jesus stepped on the scene everything changed. Those who could not walk were now walking with a new pep in their step.

Those who could not see were now seeing with better than 20/20 vision. Those who could not talk couldn't shut up about what Jesus had done for them.

One lady had been dealing with a blood issue for seven years, but when she touched the hem of His garment, she was healed. You see, there was no physical ailment or disease that could withstand His healing touch, but His healing touch didn't just stop with extreme medical conditions, it reached into the deepest emotional and spiritual realm as well, and in there, there was no demon or sin that could over-power His command.

He could calm the most terrifying storms with a simple, "Be still." He could walk on the water as if it were paved with freshly laid asphalt. He had a built in Omniscient Fish Finder Radar that knew exactly where the best fishing spots were. Speaking of fish, who doesn't like a good old-fashioned fish fry? Jesus served a meal to 5,000 people with just five loaves of bread and two fish.

The Bible even tells of the time that Jesus raised a man named Lazarus, who had been dead for 4 days, from the dead! The religious experts really got mad about that one! There was just no limit to the power of Jesus Christ, and He hasn't weakened one bit. No wonder Mark tells us, "So when the centurion, who stood opposite Him, saw that He cried out like this and breathed His last, he said, 'Truly this Man was the Son of God!' (Mark 15:39). His power was evident! His power was undeniable! Even as He was in His most vulnerable position facing His greatest opposition, death.

Yet, some who were in attendance that day still chose not to believe. The same is true today!

The Gospel of Mark is a constant refreshed feed of the life, death, burial, and resurrection of Jesus Christ. It jumps from one spot to the next, one topic to the next, one miracle to the next. It's pretty brief but to the point. If you haven't already, let me encourage you to take some time and read the Gospel of Mark.

In just sixteen chapters, Mark describes the service of Jesus and His sacrifice in breathtaking fashion, seeming to leave us wanting more and more. "Jesus goes there." "Jesus did this." "Jesus did that." You can feel Mark's excitement as you read his account. I love it!

Jesus continues to prove throughout the Scriptures that He is all-powerful, all-knowing, everywhere, and eternal. In fact, He was proving exactly who He was so there would be no doubt in anyone's mind. He was God in the flesh! He came to express the love of God. He came to do the works that only God could do. He came to give us a choice: to believe or not to believe. He came displaying the power of God, boldly proclaiming, "I Am."

In Mark chapter 9 we see the pinnacle of this spiritual agenda. Starting in verse 14 we find Jesus walking into a "religious discussion" between His disciples and the Scribes. The Scribes were a part of the historic elites of the era. They would have been considered quite the religious "know it alls."

In this passage we are reminded that until Jesus is at the center of the discussion and we run our ideas through the Jesus account filter, we can't come to any true answers. All too often, our conclusions will only bring more confusion.

So, Jesus walks up and says, "What are you guys talking about?"

One in the crowd speaks up, "I brought You my son who has a mute spirit, it controls him, throws him down to the ground, he foams at the mouth, gnashes his teeth and becomes unmovable. I asked your disciples to cast the demon out but they couldn't."

Jesus responds, and when He responds, He doesn't just address the man but He addresses all around Him, and, He answered him and said, "O, faithless generation, how long shall I be with you? How long shall I bear with you? Bring him to Me" (Mark 9:19).

They bring the young man to Jesus and when the boy locks eyes on Jesus, the demon threw the boy to the ground, he began convulsing, screaming, and foaming at the mouth. Jesus asks, "How long has this been happening to him?" The dad responds, "since his childhood, he's been thrown into the fire and into the water by it, the demon has tried to kill him over and over." Now, this is vital, do not miss this! The man then says, "And often he has thrown him both into the fire and into the water to destroy him. But if You can do anything, have compassion on us and help us" (Mark 9.22).

"Jesus said to him, "If you can believe, *all things are possible to him who believes*" (Mark 9:23). Immediately, the father of the child cried out and said with tears, "Lord, I *believe*; help my unbelief!" (Mark 9:24).

I bet you can guess what happens next, something amazing, something awesome, something... impossible! For this hurting dad: Anything? Turned into, anything! Immediately, Jesus healed the young man because of this statement, "Lord, I believe!" God specializes in turning "anything?" Into "anything!"

3

Anything!

Testifying to Jews, and also to Greeks, repentance
toward God and faith toward our Lord Jesus Christ.
(Acts 20:21)

W ithout grace there is no salvation. Without
faith there is no salvation. Without the
grace of God reaching down to us for salvation and

us having faith in His Son Jesus Christ, there is no salvation.

The only combination better than peanut butter and jelly is grace and faith. Grace is a gift from God. The grace of God is amazing and none of us deserves His grace; yet He gives it to us. Equally important is our faith. Our faith in God starts with our response to His grace.

Faith is vital to the sustainability of the Christian life. Faith and trust go hand in hand. Faith in God propels our spiritual life into action. We become alive in Jesus Christ by our faith! Works will always follow our faith.

Ephesians chapter 2 says, "For by grace you have been saved through faith, and that not of yourselves; it is the gift of God, not of works, lest anyone should boast" (Eph. 2:8–9). Grace is God's unmerited, unearned, undeserved favor to all mankind. God's grace saves us, but grace becomes our possession by faith, and that faith is a gift from God in the being of Jesus Christ. Let me simplify this for us all: grace was God's choice; faith is our choice!

Let me say that again a little louder for the people in the back.

Grace was and is God's choice; faith will always be our choice!

Grace reaches down. Faith reaches up.

Take notes on this, highlight this, underline this, circle this. Nobody who has ever cried out for salvation has ever been denied by God. Please do not accuse God of saving some and rejecting others. Salvation is for all who will come to God in believing faith, trusting Jesus as their personal Savior. Now, of course, we know no matter how unfortunate it is, not all will call on Christ for salvation. I wish they would, but it's just not the case. Many will reject, many will not believe that God loved the world so much that He gave *(grace)* His only begotten Son *(Jesus)*. Whoever *(You, Me, Them, Anyone)* believes In Him *(faith)* will not perish *(hell)* but have everlasting life *(heaven)*. Thank God, for His grace! Thank God, for Jesus!

The combination of grace and faith saves us. Salvation now becomes our new identity and reality. We shouldn't just talk about our faith, or debate the things of faith, or try to abide by our articles of faith, but we should live every moment, every hour, every day by faith! We should be men and women of faith, believing that with God all things are possible. Faith in God fuels our souls with heavenly power straight from the throne of God himself. The reality of our relationship with God or lack thereof, completely hinges on our faith in God. Our faith in God expresses our love for God.

One of my favorite books on the topic of faith was written by Dr. Ed Hindson. The book is titled, *Courageous Faith: Life Lessons from Old Testament Heroes.* Once you're finished with this book, check out that one, you will love the in-depth study from the Old Testament characters and the stories about how their faith carried them through life. In that book Dr. Hindson makes this statement on the importance of having faith in God, he writes,

> The power of our faith rests in the object of our faith. At the foundation of all love is a belief in the object that is loved. If I do not believe in a person, I cannot love him. The same is true in our relationship with God. Without faith it is impossible for us to know Him or love Him. Faith is the starting point in our spiritual journey. We must begin with God: believing that He exists, believing that He cares, and believing that His love is real.

Faith in God propels us into action; it is the first step in our spiritual journey. God can do anything! Nothing unleashes the power of love in our lives like our faith in God. God can do anything! Nothing brings joy to the Father's heart like a child who trusts in Him. God can do anything!

Nothing Unleashes The Power Of God In Our Lives Like Our Faith

Everything comes down to faith in God and faith in His Word.

In the beginning God created the heavens and the earth? God can do anything.

"Noah, build a boat. A big boat. About four football fields long?"

I can do anything.

"Sarah, I know you're ninety years old, but it's time you have a baby?"

Umm. Don't laugh! I can do anything.

Are you getting the point? Just in case you're not, I'll keep going. How about David and Goliath? God can do anything. Shadrach, Meshach, and Abednego...God can do anything. Daniel checks in to The Lion Plaza Hotel—by the way it had terrible reviews. God can do anything. Here's a good one, Jonah survives being swallowed by a "great fish." A giant bluegill, largemouth bass, a whale, mosasaurs? Who cares? It doesn't matter. What matters is the

Bible, the Word of God, is driving home the point that God really can do anything.

If God prepared a bluegill to swallow up Jonah, that's exactly what swallowed up Jonah. "Now the Lord had prepared a great fish to swallow Jonah." (Jonah 1:17)

You know why it was called a "great fish?" Because God prepared it. God does great things. He does God things. He does mighty things beyond our imaginations. God does the impossible. God can do anything.

Either God Can Do Anything Or He Can't

Mary was a virgin. She was not sexually active. She had never had sexual intercourse. God can do anything. Do you see the significance of this statement that is found in Luke 1:37? Do you sense the power behind it? Either God can do anything or He can't. If He can, He is the One True God and there is no other. If He can't, then He is a complete and utter forgery, but the God of the Bible *can* do anything! He exceeds all limits. As believers of Jesus Christ, we really have no reason to doubt Him.

Faith is what our entire religion is built on! It is not based on works, it is not based on sacraments, it is not based on baptism, it is not based on sincerity, or promises made to appease an ancient deity. Christianity is built on faith. It is built on a concrete foundation, found in the birth, life, death, resurrection, and soon return of our Lord and Savior Jesus Christ.

This is what all of Christianity revolves around. Jesus makes the severity of our faith crystal clear. John 8 says, "Therefore I said to you that you will die in your sins; for if you do not believe that I Am He, you will die in your sins" (John 8:24). No forgiveness, no heaven, no life at its very best without the pollution of sin; a decision must be made whether to have faith in Jesus or not.

Maybe now more than ever, we have been given every reason under heaven to live courageous and optimistic lives! God has proven over and over again that He can do anything. The Bible gives us multiple examples of Him doing the impossible; this should give us great confidence during the times when we seem to be facing the impossible.

In order for God to make the impossible possible, we must have faith! We must believe. We must fully trust God. We must lay aside all doubts, no matter how rational or reasonable they appear to be. We are to walk by faith not by sight. We must stop believing everything that we see going on around us and we must live our lives based on what God's Word says not what we see. We walk by faith by trusting God, His Word, and the leading of His Holy Spirit!

The more our faith in God develops, the more our life begins to mature in the direction God wants it to go. Faith is spiritual but it's also practical!

There is a story found in the Bible tucked away in the Old Testament about a man named Job. Job was a man of faith, many around him would have dubbed him faithful. Job was also a man of well-deserved prosperity. He was a godly man, extremely wealthy, a good husband, a good father. He really had it all together!

Then, in a moment, in a drastic chain of events, Job's life changed forever, and he lost everything and was surrounded by brokenness, loss, and grief. He lost it all. He was now bankrupt, homeless, helpless, and childless, but he was never hopeless. As Job and his wife stood over brand-new graves that held their children, Job leans over on her and says, "Naked I came from my mother's womb, and naked shall I return there. The Lord gave, and the Lord has taken away; Blessed be the name of the Lord" (Job 1:21).

Her response must have been a total shock to him! Mrs. Job was not tracking what Job was saying. Her response was quite different, not nearly as convincing, downright faithless, and even more devastating to Job's crushed spirit. Scripture tells us, "Then his wife said to him, 'Do you still hold fast to your integrity? Curse God and die!'" (Job 2:9). Talk about adding insult to injury? Job's friends then come to him and don't offer much hope or help either, and as the story goes Job seeks God for answers but he only finds silence. I won't take time to go into all the details, but thankfully the story has a happy ending. You know why? Because all stories of people who have faith in God have a happy ending! The future is always bright with Jesus Christ!

God breaks His silence, speaks a word of hope, promise, and fulfillment into Job's life. Then God rewards Job for his faith and faithfulness far greater than Job ever had to begin with. You know what I find so interesting about this entire story? At one point Job cried out to God and said, "My spirit is broken, My days are extinguished; The grave is ready for me." (Job 17:1)

All Stories of People Who Have Faith in God Have a Happy Ending

Those are some incredibly strong, and deeply emotional words from a hurting and disappointed person. There's a lot Job didn't know. There was a lot he didn't understand. He had no clue why one day, completely out of the blue, the bottom dropped out, tornadoes, storms, fires, destruction, death...it all changed in a moment. All his life Job walked with God, he had been faithful, he had been obedient, he had been submissive, and now this. He asked the question we all have asked before, "Why do bad things happen to good people?"

On and on it goes: tomorrow is worse than today, but in the heat of the battle, Job makes an bold statement, a real proclamation of his faith when he says, "He knows the way that I take, when He has tested me, I shall come forth as gold" (Job 23:10). Job refers to himself as coming through all this "stuff" as pure, precious, and powerful as gold. He says, "God knows all about it." He says, "God is allowing this into my life." He says, "After these trials have ended, God will bless me in a unique way. In fact, I will be better than I was before. There will be blessings that will follow all this because my trust is in God." You see, Job's faith was in God. This is a pretty remarkable reminder for us all. Job doesn't deny the trials, but he knows there is hope beyond them.

Job chapter 2 says, "But he said to her, 'You speak as one of the foolish women speaks. Shall we indeed accept good from God, and shall we not accept adversity?' In all this Job did not sin with his lips" (Job 2:10). What faith Job had! We are not just supposed to have faith in God when things are good; we are supposed to have faith in God when things are not so good. He is our God when things are bad and when things are going awesome.

Our faith in Him isn't limited to those days He blesses us. We don't get to claim Him as our Lord only when we get what we want. He is God of all gods, and Lord of all lords, even when adversity strikes. God can do anything! He won't leave us on the day we start suffering, Job was spot on! Talk about a great faith! Talk about a person who *believed* that God could do anything!

One of my favorite verses in all Scripture says, "That the genuineness of your faith, being much more precious than gold that perishes, though it is tested by fire, may be found to praise, honor, and glory at the revelation of Jesus Christ" (1 Peter 1:7).

Our faith is more important than anything we could accumulate on this earth.

Our possessions won't make it to eternity. Our cars, our boats, our homes will all stay here on this earth after we're gone.

Our money, our clothes will all stay here, but we will go on, we will live on. We all will live forever, and the most important thing we possess as believers in Christ—more precious than any amount of gold—is our faith. Nothing is more important in this life than having faith in God.

4

Consequences of Unbelief

Then He said to Thomas, "Reach your finger here,
and look at My hands; and reach your hand here,
and put it into My side. Do not be unbelieving,
but believing." (John 20:27)

There's a passage of Scripture that has always
been troubling to me. It can be found in
Matthew 13and it says, "Now He did not do many
mighty works there because of their unbelief" (Matt.

13:58). Wait...What? Hold up! For three full chapters I've been saying Jesus was God in the flesh, and God can do anything.

He is part of the Holy Trinity, God the Father, God the Son and God the Holy Spirit. He is all-powerful, all-knowing, everywhere. So, what's going on? I thought, with God, all things were possible? God can do anything, right? As Christians we are supposed to believe this, as a follower of Jesus Christ, I believe the answer to all these questions is an absolute, resounding, YES! So how could we now be reading in His very own book, the Bible, that He is being limited to what He does. How can this be? Can mere finite human beings limit an all-powerful God?

Nowhere in Scripture can we find God limiting Himself, and He is the same yesterday, today, and forever. His miracle working power hasn't changed. So, why didn't He do many mighty works there? The answer to that question is found in the same text in the clause, "Because of their unbelief." Notice it wasn't because of their lack of finances or because there were no issues or problems in that area. He didn't do many mighty works there because of their lack of faith.

I guess the reason I find this passage of Scripture so troubling is that this passage expresses that there are eternal effects of lives lived without faith in Jesus Christ. However, the passage reassures us that there are also blessings beyond human comprehension through faith and there are equally scarcity and curses without faith.

The lack of faith recorded here in Matthew 13 literally stops the miracles of God. Let's make it real. Let me get in your grill for a second. Our lack of faith limits the miracles of God! Your lack of faith limits the miracles of God in your life and in the lives of those close to you.

There Are Eternal Effects Of Lives Lived Without Faith

My lack of faith limits the miracles of God. Our families' lack of faith and our churches' lack of faith— our staffs', our boards'—will limit the work of God in our communities. Lack of faith, unbelief, is exactly what is limiting the miracles of God in all areas of our lives. That's right, you read that 100 percent correctly, but just in case you skipped it or had to check your phone to see if it was still working, please go back and read it again, slowly and maybe out loud.

Our Lack of Faith Limits The Miracles Of God

Our lack of faith limits the miracles of God. Etched in the Scriptures for us to read is the proof of how detrimental our lack of faith is to our world. When we choose to not believe, we are missing out on so much. We are missing out on all God desires to do in our lives! The Bible makes it clear that He would not do any great work there "because of their lack of faith." Notice it doesn't say that "He was unable" or that "He couldn't," but it says, "He would not!"

Do you see how significant this passage is? Unfortunately, all too often it gets overlooked! I have no doubt that there was work that God wanted to do for the people in that area but their faith was nonexistent. It was God's desire to do something more. He was searching for an opportunity. He was searching for faith, yet He only found unbelief. It was His desire to do more. God wants to pour out His blessings. He could have rocked their world with all different types of miraculous works, but He didn't, and the reason He didn't, was because of their unbelief.

We see in the Gospel of Mark, "And He marveled because of their unbelief. Then He went about the villages in a circuit, teaching" (Mark 6:6). This is not the "ooh-ahh" type of marveling. This is a displeasure, shock! Our unbelief in God is unbeliev-able to Him. Not only was He unwilling to do mighty works there, but He was truly amazed and disgusted by their lack of faith!

Our Unbelief Is Unbelievable to God

God doesn't get surprised, or shocked, by any-thing, but there is a real shock and disgust with man-kind that is seen in this passage and it's because of their lack of faith in Him. I am thankful for the patience God shows to us. I am thankful for the patience God shows to me. You should be thankful for His mercy and patience, but His greatest desire for all of us is that we have faith in Him. He wants us trust Him. It is His desire to do something great in our lives but He is waiting on our faith to get the blessing ball rolling.

It is faith that opens up the floodgates of God's grace. I'm so glad that 2 Peter says, "The Lord is not slack concerning His promise, as some count slack-ness, but is longsuffering toward us, not willing that any should perish but that all should come to repentance" (2 Peter 3:9). Our faith activates God's grace in our everyday life. Regardless of who you are, where you came from, or even what you have been doing, by God's grace and through faith you can become a child of God. God is patient and longsuffering with each and every one of us. He continues to show us mercy every morning, any day we spend not living by faith it truly displeases Him, because He can do anything!

Not only does our unbelief limit His work in our lives, but it also hinders His work in our communities. I believe our culture is in major crisis because our churches have a faith problem. For too long we have put our faith in our finances, formalities, fabrications instead of having faith in a God that can do anything. The children of Israel struggled with this all throughout the Old Testament, and in one instance from Joshua 5:6 we know they walked in the wilderness for forty years because of it. In the New Testament, the theme continues with statements from Jesus Christ in the Gospels, and reiterated by the Apostle Paul in his epistles like Ephesians 4:5-6 when he writes, "One Lord, one faith, one baptism, one God and Father of all, who is above all, and through all, and in you all." Faith in God connects us, it propels us to action and it builds strong communities.

Think back to the very beginning of it all. In the garden of Eden, Adam and Eve had a choice: have faith in God and have faith in His word or believe the words of a snake. We all know how that worked out for them, for us, and for all of creation. Human beings were forever thrown from paradise, and the curses of death and disease infecting the entire world were handed out. Oh yeah, and my personal favorite: working in the heat of the day sweating like a hog in a microwave.

God was not happy. In fact, He was extremely disgusted with Adam and Eve, and His judgement was on the way. Why? Some would say, "Disobedience," and that's a good answer. But I would argue there's an even better answer than that. I would suggest, what broke His heart was their unbelief in Him. It was their unbelief the cost them everything. That's why He was so upset with them. They doubted God's promise. They doubted His word. They didn't believe. They didn't trust Him.

Their lack of faith led to their disobedience, which ultimately lead to death spiritually and eventually to a physical death. Our lack of faith in God will always lead to disobedience, and disobeying God and His word will always move us away from His presence, power, and peace. This is what God defines as "sin," and why we know this case, the first sin, as the original sin. At the root of sin is really an original separation from God and His blessings that is the result of lack of faith.

Our Lack Of Faith In God Will Always Lead To Disobedience

If Satan can get you doubting God's word, He can get you debating His word, reasoning your way out of it. If you're doubting God's word, you're not going to obey it. God was Adam and Eve's source of life. He was what all their faith was in. He was their eternal source of provision and supplies. They knew this, they believed it...until they didn't! And once they doubted, everything changed. That's exactly what our sin does now, it separates us from the presence of God.

Adam and Eve immediately realized they had disconnected from life itself, and fear entered into their hearts. It was all caused because of the original unbelief, "but of the fruit of the tree which is in the midst of the garden, God has said, 'You shall not eat it, nor shall you touch it, lest you die'" (Gen. 3:3).

In that verse, Adam and Eve even quoted God! They knew His word but they didn't truly believe it. We too can know His Word, but if we don't believe it and allow that belief to guide our choices, our knowledge is worthless.

No matter how much Bible you know or have memorized, it is worthless if you don't truly believe it. Adam and Eve knew exactly what He had told them. They knew the truth, yet for a moment in time they believed they were missing out on something. They doubted that God had their best interests in mind. "Then the serpent said to the woman, 'You will not surely die. For God knows that in the day you eat of it your eyes will be opened, and you will be like God, knowing good and evil'" (Gen. 3:4–5).

No Matter How Much Bible You Know Or Have Memorized, It's All Worthless If You Don't Truly Believe It

Adam and Eve didn't believe God, they believed a stranger, and their unbelief in God's word cost them everything. It cost them God's protection, God's provision, and most importantly God's presence. That unbelief caused God to hand out serious consequences. They had been given permission to eat from any tree in the garden except one—any tree at all, yet they were convinced there was more. They were certain they were missing out on something by simply trusting God for every area of their lives.

They were tricked into believing they had been tricked by God. They believed that there was something out there, somewhere, and they were missing out on it by fully trusting in God. They wanted their eyes to be opened; they wanted to be gods. I believe many continue to strive to be gods.

Can I just say, we don't need to be gods and goddesses, God has it covered? He has never asked us to be anything more than faithful to Him, to trust Him, to believe Him, to know He is all we need. This is what it means to be a man or woman of faith. We must be men and women of faith if we seek the blessing of God's grace in our lives. "Moreover it is required in stewards that one be found faithful" (1 Cor. 4:2). We must believe with all of our hearts, all of our souls, and all of our minds that God can do anything.

Our faith is a direct reflection of our love for God. Our works are a direct reflection of our faith in God. Our faith causes great changes in our lives. Our faith spawns growth and improvement. Our faith taps into the blessings of heaven.

Being faithful starts with believing that God can do anything. God will always reward our faith.

God will always reward our faithfulness and there are always consequences to our unbelief. Unbelief causes us to miss out on the blessings of God. We see God offer His blessings all throughout Scripture and each of those blessings are given by His grace and distributed according to our faith. One of my personal favorites is found in Romans 5, where the Apostle Paul expresses the greatest gift of all offered to us by God Himself, "Therefore, having been justified by faith, we have peace with God through our Lord Jesus Christ" (Rom. 5:1). We receive peace with God through our faith in Jesus Christ.

Unbelief also strips us from the presence of God. Adam and Eve were removed from the garden of Eden. Their disobedience, their unbelief in God's word, and their sin separated them from God. The same is true with us. When we don't believe God can do anything, we drift from His presence. Belief in God drives us closer to Him.

Unbelief blinds us from appreciating where and how God is working in our lives. When we don't believe that God can do anything, we miss out on seeing Him move in every situation. We miss out on experiencing His goodness even in the most difficult seasons of life. A person filled with faith is evident to the world around them, but so is a person whose life is filled with unbelief. Faith is evident in our lives and so is unbelief. Faith is contagious and so is unbelief. Ask yourself which are you spreading?

Our faith in God will pour out in every area of life, and unfortunately so will our lack of faith. This world desperately needs men and women of God to cling to that everlasting promise that was proclaimed to Mary and boldly proclaim, "Yes! God can do anything"

Just for a moment, as we close this chapter out, think of the impact it would make on your life if you truly believed that God can do anything. Consider all the ways in which your life would have been different if you filtered every idea, every thought, every word, every action through that one single truth from God's Word. Think too of the consequences and effects on your own life that you have witnessed or experienced because of unbelief.

5

Fear and Unbelief

Then Philip said, "If you believe with all your heart, you may." And he answered and said, "I believe that Jesus Christ is the Son of God." (Acts 8:37)

S ince we looked at the beginning of the Bible, let's fast forward to the end. Did you know the Bible gives us prophetic insight on who will spend eternity separated from God's presence in a place called hell, which is a place prepared for Satan but also a place where those who reject the grace of God will eventually end up?

The list is found in Revelation 21, and here's what God's Word describes, "But the cowardly, unbelieving, abominable, murderers, sexually immoral, sorcerers, idolaters, and all liars shall have their part in the lake which burns with fire and brimstone, which is the second death" (Rev. 21:8).

So let's work though this list, and work from back to front.

#8. *Liars.* Liars will be in hell. Makes sense, right? Those who lie do not know the truth. Jesus is the way, the truth, and the life. Jesus proclaims this in John 14 when He said this to His disciples, "I am the way, the truth, and the life. No one comes to the Father except through Me" (John 14:6). People who believe the truth won't be in hell; however, those who believe lies and who offer lies, will be in hell.

If those in hell would have believed the truth and lived the truth found in Jesus Christ, they would have never found themselves in that horrible place.

I have a hard time having patience to deal with a liar. Lying is so degrading to the person receiving the information. Liars have no respect for anyone they speak their lies to and no remorse about their knowing attempt to mislead them. I have had people lie to me and it hurts so bad. Let's be honest, does anyone really like a liar?

According to the Bible, hell will be filled with liars. What a terrible place to spend eternity. I wonder what lies will be repeated over and over in the ears of the occupants forever and ever. Maybe it will be the words of false prophets, or maybe the words of false religions, or the words of news reporters or of bloggers mocking the Bible and the things of God, or the lie that hell isn't so bad and all your friends will be there too. Hell will be a place completely void of the truth.

#7. *Idolaters.* Those in hell have worshiped false gods all their lives. Idolaters from all time will be in hell, whether they worshiped a tree, a monkey, a crystal, a sculpture, a drug, a politician, a sport, or money and power. Over and over again, the Bible makes clear the dangers of idolatry.

The Prophet Isaiah is just one person God has used to address this issue in Isaiah 45:20 where he writes, "Assemble yourselves and come; Draw near together, You who have escaped from the nations. They have no knowledge, Who carry the wood of their carved image, And pray to a god that cannot save" (Isa. 45:20).

Idolatry Is Spitting in the Face of the Creator of the Universe, While Worshipping Something in Our Hands That We Have Created

In that chapter alone it's stated multiple times that there is only one God who can save and He can't be made or controlled by human hands. Idolatry takes God from His rightful place and places Him down to our level. Idolatry is spitting in the face of the creator of the universe while worshipping something in our hands that we have created. Idolatry abandons the way that God has laid out for us in His Word for our own lustful pursuits. People in hell loved their idols more than anything else. They put their faith in their idols instead of having faith in Jesus Christ.

The idolater says, "I choose who or what I worship." Many in our world today live for and chase after things they can hold in their own hands instead of pursuing the things of God and a relationship with Him. Idolaters are filled with hate because they're always chasing after more. Hell will be filled with people who won't be able to fulfill their greatest desires.

#6. *Sorcerers.* Sorcery follows idolatry. With lies in the mouth, idols in one hand, magic, spells, jewels, powders, bones, teeth, hair, and rings in the other, sorcerers are described biblically as those who practice witchcraft, using and gaining power given by demons and evil spirits. Sorcery is the act of using spells, chanting, chatting to spirits, which is all defined as an abomination in God's eyes.

Second Chronicles 33 describes a man wrapped up in sorcery, his name was Manasseh and he was a king of Jerusalem. It says, "Also he caused his sons to pass through the fire in the Valley of the Son of Hinnom; he practiced soothsaying, used witchcraft and sorcery, and consulted mediums and spiritists. He did much evil in the sight of the Lord, to provoke Him to anger" (2 Chron. 33:6).

God never, ever approves of witchcraft or sorcery. He never did in the Bible and He hasn't changed His mind on the topic. No matter how many sections of materials related to witchcraft are set up in your local bookstore, or how many movies and TV shows do their best to normalize it, hell will be filled with witches and warlocks throughout all of time.

What is comical or entertaining about witches, vampires, ghost, zombies? Why do we struggle with the fact that Satan continues to normalize and popularize these abominations in our culture?

Death, darkness, torture, spells, are not things to be played with.

Shouts of fear will echo through the extreme heat and stink of burning sulfur. Ear piercing screams will light up the darkness, with no relief or let up, and no hope of light in sight. Moans and groans of grueling pain will echo through the pits of hell, with no laughter, no joy, just curses and unfulfilled rage.

#5. *The Sexually Immoral.* Here, sexually immoral can be interchanged for terms such as, *fornicator* or *adulterer.* The original language uses the word, *pornos,* which is tied to *porneia,* which we would recognize as the root of the word *pornography.*

It's no secret, we live in a society saturated with sex, and hell will be filled with those whose lives have been controlled by their sexual lust, those lost in their lust for anyone or anything, those who worshiped sex above all.

Jesus addresses this topic and takes it even a step further on the dangers of lust, sexual immorality, and not having self-control in our passions. We find His words in Matthew 5, when He says, "But I say to you that whoever looks at a woman to lust for her has already committed adultery with her in his heart" (Matt. 5:28).

Jesus makes it clear that our lust starts in the heart not with the eyes. Those who burn with lust in this life, will never find peace in the life to come.

#4 *Murderers.* God is the creator of life. I believe you and I have been created in the image and likeness of God. When a person murders another person, they are destroying that which was created by God Himself. When Adam and Eve opened the door for sin to enter the Garden of Eden, death entered in right behind it. A spiritual death occurred, they were now separated from God. However, a physical death would now become their reality as well. Their son Cain would ultimately be the first murderer in the history of all mankind.

His hatred toward his own brother, and disobedience towards God brought murder into the world. Cain tried to worship God on his own terms not God's terms. Abel obeyed God's word and pleased God, which caused his brother to hate him. So Cain lured his brother into the woods, trying to hide his evil intents, he took a rock and murdered Abel. Murder is fueled by hate. I have never heard of anyone who loved someone to a physical death.

The Bible says in 1 John 4:8, "He who does not love does not know God, for God is love." God is love. Jesus makes it very clear that we should, love

God and love one another. This is a commandment given by God. Understanding the worth of a human life is one of the ways we honor, love and respect God and His creation. Don't Hate God. Don't Hate Others. Murder is a political issue, but even greater than that it's a biblical issue. Sin brings death. But there's good news, Jesus Christ says in Matthew 5:21-22 "You have heard that it was said to those of old, 'You shall not murder, and whoever murders will be in danger of the judgment.' But I say to you that whoever is angry with his brother without a cause shall be in danger of the judgment. And whoever says to his brother, 'Raca!' shall be in danger of the council. But whoever says, 'You fool!' shall be in danger of hell fire."

Then the one who spoke these words, Jesus, is taken and hung on a cross to be murdered by the world, hanging between Heaven and Earth, and among His final words were, "Father, forgive them." Jesus died so that even murderers could be forgiven. Jesus rose from the grave, conquering death, so that God's final word was not murder but resurrection and life!

#3. *Abominable.* Merriam-Webster defines abominable as, "worthy of or causing disgust or hatred:

very bad, unpleasant." In most relatable terminology, hell will be filled with the kind of people who you saw when turned on the news and saw a story about which you just shook your head and thought, "How could anyone do that to someone else?" Or, "Why would anyone do that?" Hell will be filled with those types of people—killers, rapists, terrorists, and racists. Hell will be filled with child molesters, sex traffickers, and predators. Hell will be filled with perverts, maniacs, and murderers. God despises these acts; God hates these actions. They are not driven by faith, hope, love, joy, peace, contentment, self-control, and kindness.

Every God rejector from the time of Adam and Eve, past present and future, will be in hell, forever and ever. Hell will be filled with the worst of the worst to ever breath on this planet. As you read this list, you were thinking of all those people who you know of that fit one, some, or all of these categories, but before we move on, go back and reread that list. It's easy to think of all "those" people as we read this list, but let's consider the last two in our discussion, the first two on the list, which will probably be more than a little more relevant.

When we consider the first two types of sinner bound for hell, we see that the Bible has a unique way of taking the unbelieving and the cowardly and combining them as one and the same or the fearful.

Have you ever been around someone who is just afraid all the time? People like this are not very fun to hang out with at all. I know people who are afraid to close their eyes to sleep. I can't imagine what that's like to deal with every night. I know people who are terrified to ride in a car. Of course, I have been a passenger with some people whose driving skills have terrified me a little bit for sure. Many people hate to fly on an airplane or even ride on a roller coaster. But when it comes right down to spiritually speaking, being fearful and unbelieving go hand in hand. Over and over again, we see God's message to all mankind remain the same, "Do not be afraid." He says this hundreds of times throughout His Word.

We hear lots of words of fear being spoken in our world today, but if we silence the words of this world, I believe we will hear Jesus say, "Fear not!" Many fear losing all their money, but Jesus says, "Fear not!" Many fear their health may be failing, but Jesus, says, "Fear not!" If we are connected to the God who can do anything, what do we truly have to fear? If we have a relationship with the God, who can do anything, what should keep us from having a faith as bold as a roaring lion?

Fear Not

In Revelation 21:8, God is warning us. He's describing the future for us. He's making it clear that we can change our eternal address from hell to heaven, from eternal pain and suffering to life at its very best without the pollution of sin. He is describing the people who will inhabit that terrible place called hell. He is not using a fear tactic. God is simply telling us the truth; He is letting us know who will end up in hell. If you listen closely, I believe you will hear Him speaking, and you know what He is saying? He is saying, "Do not be afraid." We don't have to live in fear. We don't have to fear life after this life.

Mary was engaged to Joseph. Before they came together, she was pregnant by the Holy Spirit. Joseph was her future husband and fully understood the issues this could cause. While he pondered all of his options, an angel of the Lord appeared to Him in a dream and the angel's opening statement to Joseph was...you want to take a guess?

It wasn't, "Stock up on diapers, and baby formula!" It was, "Do not be afraid."

"Joseph, son of David, do not be afraid to take to you Mary your wife, for that which is conceived in her if of the Holy Spirit" (Matt. 1:20).

Do you remember the story of Jesus walking on the water? It's found in Matthew 14, where it says,

> But the boat was now in the middle of the sea, tossed by the waves, for the wind was contrary. Now in the fourth watch of the night Jesus went to them, walking on the sea. And when the disciples saw Him walking on the sea, they were troubled, saying, "It is a ghost!" And they cried out for fear. But immediately Jesus spoke to them, saying, "Be of good cheer! It is I; *do not be afraid.*" (Matthew 14:24–27 emphasis added NKJV)

The disciples were in a boat a long way from shore, struggling against the wind and waves. They were alone. It was dark, and Jesus was nowhere to be found. But Jesus was closer than they knew. God is always closer to us than we realize. Jesus had His eyes on them the entire time. He began walking on the water in their direction, and when His disciples saw Him walking on the water, they were even more terrified.

They began to scream, "It's a ghost! It's a ghost! We're all doomed." Jesus heard their cries and immediately spoke to them and said, want to guess? He didn't say, "Boo!" He didn't say, "I am a ghost!" He said, "Do not be afraid." Peter yelled back, "Lord, if it's you let me come out and walk with you on the water." Jesus said, "Come on out." Peter stepped out of the boat and walked on the water in the direction of Jesus.

Just a few seconds before, Peter was screaming, "We're all going to die."

And in an instant, He was walking on water! This is without a doubt one of the greatest acts of faith ever recorded in Scripture. Why? Because he heard the words of Jesus and believed the words of Jesus. He knew exactly who was doing the talking. Yet, when he felt the wind on his face and saw the waves, the Bible says, "He was once again, frightened." And Peter began to sink.

The water covered his ankles and then his knees. Peter was no longer in control. Bigger waves than ever were coming in his direction, the wind was beating against his face, and his heart rate accelerated. He was no longer just scared; he was terrified and without help he would not survive. He drew enough strength to cry out from the darkness, "Lord, save me!" (Matt. 14:25–30 author's paraphrase NKJV)

And you know what Jesus did? He saved Him.

What a perfect illustration of salvation. Grace reaches down. Faith reaches up.

We have been given an amazing a promise: that Jesus never turns a deaf ear to a cry for help. If you would just humble yourself and cry out for help, Jesus will help you the same way He helped Peter. Whatever help you need, Jesus is more than able to help because God can do anything!

Jesus reached out His hand and grabbed Peter, and said, "Oh you of little faith, why did you doubt?" (Matt. 14:31).

You see, doubt and unbelief are the opposite of faith. Jesus was asking, why did your faith waver in me? Why did you doubt me? Why did you not take me at my word? I told you to come out on the water with me. Faith in Christ points us to life everlasting and fear and unbelief always go hand in hand.

Fear and unbelief point us in a direction away from God. Fear and faith cannot coexist in the same heart. All of Christianity is based on faith in Jesus

Christ. "For God so loved the world that He gave His only begotten Son [Jesus] that whosoever believes in Him will not perish but have everlasting life" (John 3:16).

Jesus Christ is the only way to salvation. Read that sentence again.

Jesus Christ is the only way to salvation. Do you believe this? Will you believe this?

God has given you the way to heaven, and it's through Jesus Christ.

God has given you the way to eternal life, and it is through Jesus Christ.

God has proven and promised to us all the same way so there's no confusion.

He has spoken to you through His Word that there is no need to be afraid...Do not fear.

In Proverbs 14 the Bible says, "There is a way that seems right to a man, But its end is the way of death" (Prov. 14:12). God made the only way. Whatever direction you're walking in, if it isn't the Jesus way, stop and look to Jesus.

All of John 3:16 hinges on that word *believe*. That word means to trust, to fully depend on, to completely rely on. To believe in Jesus Christ means you accept the fact you are lost in your own ways. It means you owe a debt of eternity that you cannot pay. It means you believe that Jesus died on the cross to pay it all and rose victoriously over death, hell, and the grave. It means you must completely trust Him for eternal life. It means the choice is up to you. God can do anything, including saving your soul from a place called hell. You see, God doesn't just require faith He demands it.

God Doesn't Just Require Faith, He Demands It

Faith in Jesus Christ means, no matter what, your salvation is in His hands. It means you have been given an all access pass to the blessings of heaven. Doesn't that sound wonderful? If you have never believed in Jesus Christ as Lord and Savior, would you do so right now. Please pray this prayer of faith, right now, and as you read these words put your trust in Jesus Christ and in Him alone.

Say,

Dear Lord, I know I am a sinner. I know I am completely lost and headed toward a terrible place that I don't want to go to. I believe You have given me a better way. The very best I know how, I believe in Jesus Christ! I believe

He lived, died, was buried and rose again. I'm trusting in Jesus as my Savior. I believe. I am a believer. Lord, help me to walk in Your way not my own. Fill me with Your Holy Spirit, thank you for saving me. In Jesus name, AMEN!

If you prayed that prayer, God heard you and has saved you! Now, your eternity is settled in heaven because God can do anything. All of heaven is rejoicing because you put your faith in Jesus Christ. So am I!

Would you please let me know that you prayed that prayer? I would love to celebrate with you and pray for you! Please send me an email: MiraclesInBetween@gmail.com

God's grace has reached down to you, and your faith has reached up to Him, and He has started to do a miracle in your life right now. The heavenly Father has birthed salvation in your soul through the gospel of Jesus Christ and the power of His Holy Spirit. Tell someone about your experience while reading this book and then maybe pass it along after you're done reading it to share the good news of what God can do in their life too.

6

Fire from a Recliner

And the apostles said to the Lord,
"Increase our faith." (Luke 17:5)

The power of God to work miracles is not, and never has been, dependent on the faith of any person. God is in need of nothing. He doesn't need our faith to accomplish anything. He doesn't need our faith to do the impossible, but I can't help but wonder how often He will not manifest His power because of the unbelief of mankind. Our faith doesn't make God do anything, but our faith kick-starts what God's grace has already provided.

The Power Of God To Work Miracles Is Not And Never Has Been Dependent On The Faith Of Any Person

God never performs any miracle simply to display His power or to appease people. He does the impossible to point people in His direction. He does mighty works to get our hearts and minds off of what we can see and get them focused on living a life filled by faith. He does it for His glory and so that every soul will catch a glimpse of His light in a dark and broken world.

The impossible does become possible by our faith but it's not for our comfort, happiness, or health. So why does God do the impossible? I believe there's many reasons but I'll try to wrap them all up in two simple thoughts.

First, I believe God does the impossible to inspire our praise and the glory.

Second, I believe God does the impossible so that we would share the power of His work with those who don't believe, that they might come to salvation through faith. Faith is so important. Over and over again God reveals the importance of having faith in Him.

We don't like anyone demanding anything, but God gives a command that demands a response. We see this in the act of salvation. We see this in our everyday living. Faith in Jesus Christ doesn't end with us trusting Him for salvation, that is really just the beginning of a life given to Jesus Christ.

When we say we are people of faith, are we really? Or is that just a nice gesture someone has given to us because we attend Sunday school, say our prayers before bed, and don't swear at the neighbor kids? Being a person of faith is so much more than religious rituals or a list of Do's and Don'ts. Authentic faith should be infused in every fiber of our spiritual DNA.

Real Faith Propels Us Into Real Action

Real faith propels us into real action. Faith is never meant to be left in a church building after Sunday morning service, real faith will be found in our daily decisions. Real faith will be found throughout all of our relationships and it will flow from our hearts and minds through the power of the Holy Spirit. Our faith in God should fluff our pillow at night and sound the alarm of Christian living each morning. Faith should shape our entire day.

Faith is what we believe about God, faith is what we do because of what we believe about God, and the Word of God forms our faith and strengthens it. His Word reveals the importance of having faith in God. His Word is the basis of what we know about Him and what we know about ourselves.

In Mark 11, Jesus makes a clear case for the eternal source of our faith. He simply says, "Have faith in God" (Mark 11:22). Here He is expressing the importance of having faith in God. Having faith in God is so important, and it can't be overstated. Faith is vital, and not just for the nonbeliever but also for the professing Christian.

Unfortunately, I fear many Christians have forgotten the importance of faith in their lives as well! Jesus, says, "Have faith in God." Take note of this, He doesn't say, have faith in your denomination.

He doesn't say, "Have faith in your parents."

He doesn't say, "Have faith in your church."

He doesn't say, "Have faith in your pastor."

He doesn't say, "Have faith in your Sunday school teacher."

He doesn't say, "Have faith in your counselor."

He doesn't say, "Have faith in your doctor."

Believe it or not, Jesus doesn't say, "Have faith in your favorite politician." (Shocker! Right?)

He boldly says, *"Have faith in God."*

Our faith should be in God and in Him alone. A real faith in Jesus Christ will change our lives. The Christian life starts with faith and it will end with faith. Make no mistake about it, if your faith doesn't start with God, there's a real uncertainty on where it ends, and where there is uncertainty there cannot be faith. Either you have faith in God or you don't have faith in God.

The Christian Life Starts with Faith and It Will End with Faith

Either you believe God can do anything or you believe God can do nothing.

Have faith in God. I have found in my life, my greatest disappointments have always stemmed from expecting too much of people, myself included, and not enough expectation from God. I have had people break their promises to me, but in Second Corinthians God's Word says, "All the promises of God in Him are Yes, and in Him Amen, to the glory of God through us" (2 Cor. 1:20). God will always keep His promises, so have faith in God.

We've all had people hurt us. We've all had people do us wrong. We've all had people disappoint us. We've all had people let us down, but our faith should never be in people. Hebrews 13 says, "The Lord is my helper, I will not fear. What can man do to me?" (Heb. 13:6). God will always help those who call on Him, so have faith in God.

I'm sure you have been left hanging, pushed out into the cold dark world of loneliness, but God reassures us in Isaiah 41, "Fear not, for I am with you; Be not dismayed, for I am your God. I will strengthen you, Yes, I will help you, I will uphold you with My righteous right hand" (Isa. 41:10). God will always be with you, so have faith in God.

Faith looks to an all-powerful, all-knowing God to provide for our every need. Faith looks to God and says, *"I can't do this on my own. I need Your help. I need Your power. I need Your provision. I need You."* God hears our faith, He responds to our faith, not because He has to, but because He wants to!

The Apostle Paul writes, "For in it the righteousness of God is revealed from faith to faith; as it is written, 'The just shall live by faith'" (Rom. 1:17). Can you tell Paul is putting some emphasis on the importance of faith? The just live by faith; we should be living by faith. The vibrant spiritual life is a life lived by faith. As born-again believers of our Lord and Savior Jesus Christ, we are to be living by faith. Too many Christians are wrapped up in living like the world, faithless and Godless.

The world is driven by living by sight not by faith. The worldly pant over things they can hold, measure, or control, but God has told us that we are to live by faith. Faith in God is so important, and whatever is not of faith is of sin. God's Word says, "But he who doubts is condemned if he eats, because he does not eat from faith; for whatever is not from faith is sin" (Rom. 14:23). Whatever is not from faith is sin? Yikes!

I've seen many preachers loosen their ties, pound the pulpit, hack and wave their hankies while shouting, "You ought not, drink, smoke or chew or run with girls that do!" Which I agree with by the way; however, I have heard very few sermons preached on Romans 14:23, and simply put, we are sinning when we don't have faith in God. God's Word makes it clear, "Whatever is not from faith is sin" (Rom. 14:23). When we don't live by faith, we are sinning against God. He wants us to be people of faith.

I have interacted with many Christians who have no faith at all. They proclaim they are Christians and are on their way to heaven, but many don't have enough faith to move a pebble let alone a mountain. It really breaks my heart. I didn't write this book to make you a better Calvinist, Wesleyan, Catholic, Baptist, or Pentecostal. I wrote this book to remind you that God can do anything. I believe many have forgotten that simple fact, and many haven't forgotten that truth, but for many who do believe simply aren't allowing that truth to saturate their lives.

Many Don't Have Enough Faith To Move A Pebble Let Alone A Mountain

I have left board meetings so disappointed and shaking my head at the lack of faith of men and women sitting around those church tables, astonished at their unbelief. I still believe God can do anything, and when we roll our eyes at that idea that God can do anything, we are sinning.

Pray all you want, sing as loud as you want, lift your hands as high as you want, shout as loud as you want, feed every homeless person in your city if you want, memorize all the psalms you want, act like you have it all together, stack your hair so high you've got to have air traffic control give you clearance, speak in every tongue you want, fill the back of your car with all the Christian decals you want, wear a shirt that says, "I love my church," every single day. Don't go here, do go there, affiliate yourself with this group of people, but not that group of people. But whatever you do or don't do, make no mistake about it, without faith in God, you are not pleasing God.

The writer of Hebrews says it like this: "But without faith it is impossible to please Him, for he who comes to God must believe that He is, and that He is a rewarder of those who diligently seek Him" (Heb. 11:6).

You can't please God without faith. I can't please God without faith.

If you are a professing Christian, don't you want to please God? Of course you do. What Christian doesn't want to please God? I have never asked a born-again believer that question, and had them respond with a "No, thank you. I'm good. I'd prefer Him to be mad at me." Our faith pleases Him. I don't know about you, but I want to please God.

When we don't believe that God can do anything, we are truly disappointing Him. I want Him to be pleased with me, and the best way I can bring pleasure to Him is to have faith in Him. You can't please God without faith. Hebrews 11:6 makes clear what pleases God, and it's not our finances, our good looks, or our good deeds.

It is impossible to please Him without faith! It's not our sweet rides, elaborate homes, or our outstanding credit score that pleases Him. Only our faith in Him pleases God!

Without faith it is impossible to please God.

Our faith expresses to God that we know He exists, we know He lives, we know He hears our prayers, and we know He is in complete control.

We can doubt everything else, but not Him. Why is faith so important? Because God says it is.

God says, we must have faith in Him.

God says, our faith justifies us in His eyes.

God says, we are told to live by faith.

God says, our faith pleases Him.

Our faith in God sends a clear message to the world that we belong to God. We are the righteousness of Christ. We can live above all the shame of this world, and we can live above the pain of this world because of our faith in Him.

We have been set free by God's grace and through our faith in Jesus Christ and because of that, we continue to live by faith. No matter what we are facing, we will face it by His grace and through our faith. No matter what we're going through, we go through it by faith.

The world may live by power, possessions, or positions, but we have been told to live by faith. All throughout the Bible we see examples of men and women living by faith. In fact, Hebrews 11 has been dubbed, "The Hall of Faith." In that passage we see some, not all, but some of what God did for people who had faith in Him. We see a list of people who believed God could do anything. And because of their faith, God did the impossible in their lives.

I love the way Warren Wiersbe describes Hebrews 11 when he writes,

The opening verses of Hebrews 11 are not a definition of faith but a description of faith...what faith does and how it works. True Bible faith is not blind optimism or a manufactured hope-so feeling. Neither is it an intellectual assent to a doctrine. Faith does certainly not consist of belief in spite of evidence! That would be superstition. True Bible faith is confident obedience to God's word despite circumstances and consequences.

What a perfect reflection of this passage of Scripture, the just live by faith! All these men and all these women truly believed. They believed by faith that with God the impossible becomes possible. They believed that God could do mighty things in their lives. They believed that God could do anything!

I'll never forget my first real job in a church. I was so excited. I was young, single, and full of energy, passion, and faith. I was so fired up for Jesus, I felt like charging the gates of hell with a squirt gun! They gave me my very own office, with my own desk and my own office executive chair. I remember, I even got my own computer that was so big it took up half of my desk, which seems funny to think about now as I write some of this book on my cell phone. The first few months were absolutely incredible. I was a Youth Pastor and I had our Student Ministry rocking in the right direction.

We were growing numerically as a church and I was riding high on a ministry high horse. Then, almost out of the blue, I found myself sitting on a miniature pony, all alone riding off into the sunset. I was in a difficult season of ministry. The Lead Pastor had left the church and the church was assigned a pastor who just clashed with me personally and in ministry philosophy. The honeymoon was over, and I felt the pressures of ministry like I had never experienced before.

I remember leaving the office one day and driving a few miles to my grandma's house, she was a widow and lived alone and I thought I would just swing in to visit. I remember walking in and sitting down on her couch. She was seated in my grandpa's old enormous rocking recliner.

My grandpa was a very large man, over 6'5" and 300 pounds. To me he was a giant in many ways, not just in stature but also in his faith. He was old-school too; I think he got up in the middle of the night and put on a suit and tie before he used the bathroom. He and my grandma spent forty-nine years in full-time ministry together. I had heard them talk about difficult times; I had seen them walk through difficult times.

That day we talked small talk, like the news and baseball. She was very wise, and somehow, she knew that I needed more than an ice-cold ginger ale and some pretzel rods. She looked up at me and said, "How's things at the church?" I sat in silence; I didn't want to answer. I didn't want to lie to my grandma, but I didn't want to stress her out. I mean she was eighty-two years old! So, I simply responded with one question. I asked, "Grandma, how did you and Grandpa do it all those years?"

I thought for sure she was going to give me a five-step plan to a successful ministry or at least a three-step plan on how to deal with deadly deacons, but she didn't. She just looked up at me and smiled with a smile filled with great joy and contentment and said these words, "Proverbs 3:5 and 6, 'Trust in the Lord with all thine heart, And lean not unto thine own understanding; In all thy ways acknowledge Him, and He shall direct thy paths." (KJV)

She only knew the King James Version; I think she was there when they translated it. Kidding, Grandma—I am only kidding.

She paused for a moment, bowed her head, then looked up and smiled with a face of gratitude and said, "This is how we made it. This is how I still make it. And this is how you will make it too, by trusting in the Lord."

I will never forget that moment, Holy Ghost fire from a recliner. In fact, in some ways that day seems like it was just yesterday, but it's been nearly twenty years since that day. Grandma is now with the one she trusted for over seventy-five years of her life, and her words continue to carry me through a lot of difficult seasons of life and ministry. The just live by faith. The way you will make it through is by trusting God. Have faith in God.

7

Grab The Bags!

A faithful man will abound with blessings, but he
who hastens to be rich will not go unpunished.
(Proverbs 28:20)

Don't you love Christmas? I do! Christmas is
all about anticipation and expectation all
wrapped up in the greatest gift given to all mankind
in Jesus Christ. I love giving gifts to people I love. I
love receiving gifts from people I love. The Christmas
story reminds us how much God loves us, provides

for us, and how He gave His Son Jesus Christ that we may have eternal life. It's the story of the Savior of all the world coming to earth as a little baby boy, wrapped up in swaddling clothes and Mary, His mother, placing Him in a manger.

I want you to picture it. Heaven came down to earth. Grace reached down and wrapped a gift of God's love in swaddling clothes and there in the hay among the sheep, the Lamb of God was placed. Just for a moment, pause and think about it.

The Christmas story is a life changer if you will believe it. Maybe now more than ever we need the hope, joy, peace, and love found in the Christmas story. For Christians, Christmas is so much more than Black Friday sales, shopping trips, pictures with Santa, awesome holiday cups from Starbucks, Hallmark movie specials, or even my personal favorite, great Christmas songs. Christmas is all about the Christ. Jesus! Emmanuel.

God is with us!

Like the lyrics from one of the most popular traditional advent hymns, which says:

> O Come, O Come, Emmanuel,
> And ransom captive Israel,

That mourns in lonely exile here,
Until the son of God appear.
Rejoice! Rejoice! Emmanuel !
Shall come to thee, O Israel.
(John Mason Neale 1818–1866, 1851)

The prophet Isaiah looked through the portals of time and proclaimed to the world hundreds of years before this moment in time when Christ would come to the earth and penned these words, "Therefore the Lord Himself will give you a sign: Behold, the virgin shall conceive and bear a Son, and shall call His name Emmanuel" (Isa. 7:14).

Jesus, the Christ...Emmanuel! Conceived by the Holy Spirit, delivered by the Virgin Mary, but given to us.

Jesus was born for us! God's gift to all mankind was given to us, to the outcast, to the lonely, to you, and to me. Yesterday was filled with darkness, but now light has come. Yesterday was filled with chains, but now freedom has come. Yesterday was hopeless, but now we have been given hope. God is with us! Not *was* with us. God *is* with us—right here, right now! This changes everything. Jesus changes everything. The meaning of Emmanuel expresses a vital message to all mankind from God Himself...He is with us*!*

I think we forget often that Jesus could have just shown up on earth at age thirty. He could have skipped being a snotty nose little kid. He could have skipped puberty! He could have skipped middle school. He could have skipped being forced to eat pot-luck dinners after church. He could have skipped driver's ed, and high school choir. But for some reason unknown to us, God wanted Him to enter the world through a human birth canal just like you and me. God took the faith of Mary to give birth to the greatest miracle of all time, Jesus the Christ. What faith Mary had!

Mary had faith. She believed God could do any-thing. Let me remind you once again of the conversation that took place in Luke,

Now in the sixth month the angel Gabriel was sent by God to a city of Galilee named Nazareth, to a virgin betrothed to a man whose name was Joseph, of the house of David. The virgin's name was Mary. And having come in, the angel said to her, "Rejoice, highly favored one, the Lord is with you; blessed are you among women!"

But when she saw him, she was troubled at his saying, and considered what manner of greeting this was. Then the angel said to her, "Do not be afraid, Mary, for you have found favor with God. And behold, you will conceive in your womb and bring forth a Son, and shall call His name Jesus. He will be great, and will be called the Son of the Highest; and the Lord God will give Him the throne of His father David. And He will reign over the house of Jacob forever, and of His kingdom there will be no end."

Then Mary said to the angel, "How can this be, since I do not know a man?"

And the angel answered and said to her, "The Holy Spirit will come upon you, and the power of the Highest will overshadow you; therefore, also, that Holy One who is to be born will be called the Son of God. Now indeed, Elizabeth your relative has also conceived a son in her old age; and this is now the sixth month for her who was called barren. For with God nothing will be impossible." (Luke 1:26–37)

Mary says, "How can this be? I am a virgin." The angel Gabriel answered, "The Holy Spirit will conceive inside you and the power of the most high God will make it happen. You'll have a son, and He will be the Son of God." Gabriel continues "your Aunt Elizabeth has become pregnant with a child in her old age too."

Mary was faced with a real choice. Mary had to make a decision. Gabriel's words demanded a response. The word of God always demands a response: believe or don't. Mary's response to this statement and to all that had been spoken to her sealed the deal: Mary's faith reached up and, in verse 38, she says, "Behold the maidservant of the Lord! Let it be to me according to your word" (Luke 1:38).

Grace reaches down. Faith reaches up.

Grace Reaches Down. Faith Reaches Up. Miracles Happen In Between

God's grace reached down; He gave Mary this beautiful, impossible, miraculous appointment. Mary's faith reached up as she accepted the challenge. Like Mary, we really have no reason to doubt. We have no reason to live without belief. We have every reason to live courageous and optimistic lives no matter our circumstances.

God has proven in the past that He can do anything. Why would we doubt that and believe our problems are too big for Him? How selfish we get with our problems, with our issues. Instead of turning them over to God, we hold on to them, thinking we can handle them on our own.

The Bible gives us multiple examples of Him doing the impossible, over and over again: stories like Moses leading the children of Israel from the bondage of Egypt; Daniel being tossed into a den of lions; David standing toe to toe with the giant Goliath. These are not just fun VBS "kids'" stories, these were real people facing really big challenges, just like you and me. We are real people facing real challenges, and the only way we will make it through them is if God's grace reaches down and our faith reaches up. God does His greatest work in impossible work environments.

We should gain strength and courage from these stories found in Scripture. The faith of Mary should give us great confidence during the times when we face the seemingly impossible in our lives, because I can assure you none of us is being asked to give birth to God's only son. Grace reaches down. Faith reaches up. We should expect Him to open up the heavens and pour out His blessings, which include but are not limited to His provision, His healing, His power, His presence, His strength, and His peace! Whatever God is handing out, I want it! He will always take care of His children.

My wife Angela has a favorite grocery store that she just has to visit on a weekly basis. Don't laugh, your wife has a favorite grocery store too. Right, ladies? I know you have one as well. Now, her favorite grocery store is not my favorite grocery store. Her store is very strange.

Let me explain. For starters your journey to this grocery store begins with putting a quarter in a chained, locked linked dispenser connected to hundreds of other shopping carts just to get your shopping cart.

You then weave your way through narrow lanes in a one-way direction; you wouldn't dare turn around and try to go the other direction because you will get death glares from all the people in the store. You then get to the checkout counter and place your items on the conveyor belt to a lady who looks like she literally hates her job, doesn't smile, and throws all your items into another cart at the end of the belt.

Then she looks up, musters up the strength to speak and says, "$158.72, cash or credit?"

But the most interesting part of this wonderful experience is that you have to bring your own bags! Every single time my wife goes to this grocery store she always says, "I gotta grab my bags."

She loads up her purple flowered bag, her cheetah print bag, and her dog print bag, and we head to the store. You know why? Because she fully expects to fill her bags with junk! I mean, necessities for our family's survival.

There have been times when we have forgotten our bags and had to turn around and go back home because she just couldn't shop without her bags; there was no way to bring the groceries home. When Mama goes shopping, she wants her bags, because she fully expects to bring things home from the store.

She gets on mission, and she wants to be pre-pared to deliver the goods to the poor and hungry souls at home (me especially). If she doesn't have her bags, she is not expecting to get anything!

Do you see where I am going with all of this? The same is true when we approach the throne of God by faith. Grace reaches down. Faith reaches up. When faith goes to God's grocery store, it always takes the bags!

When Faith Goes to God's Grocery Store It Always Takes the Bags

The Apostle Paul describes it this way as he wrote to the early Ephesians:

That Christ may dwell in your hearts through faith; that you, being rooted and grounded in love, may be able to comprehend with all the saints what is the width and length and depth and height—to know the love of Christ which passes knowledge; that you may be filled with all the fullness of God.

Now to Him who is able to do exceedingly abundantly above all that we ask or think, according to the power that works in us, to Him be glory in the church by Christ Jesus to all generations, forever and ever. Amen. (Ephesians 3:17–21)

Paul faced many challenges. He was snake bit, shipwrecked, beaten, hungry, sick, thrown in jail, yet he still wrote those words believing, knowing, and fully expecting it to be true in his life and in the life of every single person who would read those words and believe them. He wrote those words from personal experience in hopes that others would believe and experience faith as well. He wrote those words to encourage us, to empower us, and to strengthen our faith. God is able to do far more than we could ever think, dream, ask, or imagine! You know why? Because God can do anything!

Faith always expects the best even though the worst seems inevitable.

Faith anticipates God doing something miraculous.

Faith participates in some type of action.

Faith believes that with God all things are possible.

And faith without works is dead.

In fact James describes faith this way, "For as the body without the spirit is dead, so faith without works is dead also" (James 2:26). James describes faith in our lives as the energy that fills our life and ignites the fuse.

We believe in Jesus Christ and that belief sets us into action. It is faith that propels us to action. The Word of God demands a response: believe or not. God wants to fill our grocery bags with the blessings of heaven, but many stay on the couch of comfort and want delivery! But God will always bless our faith!

In 2019 I witnessed something I had never seen before. We had just wrapped up merging three churches, two different denominations, into one church at two different locations, and I had been installed as a Campus Pastor. It was a nice warm sunny day in North Central Ohio, and by the way those are pretty few and far between. I had driven to our main campus in Wadsworth, Ohio, for our weekly staff meeting. I was there before anyone else, so I came in and sat down at the conference table in our Lead Pastor's office.

I began looking through our visitors' names from the past Sunday and looking over my notes from the service as well. Not long after that, our Lead Pastor came in the front doors, walked in the room, put his briefcase and mail on the desk, and sat down. We exchanged pleasantries and then I proceeded to dive into all the things that were going on at our campus and all the things I wanted to get done at our campus. I was pretty fired up, so I was talking a lot.

I continued to talk and I heard him begin to open up the mail, I wasn't looking at him because my eyes were focused on my notes as I expressed my ideas.

"We want to do this."

"We need to do that."

"Where was this person on Sunday?"

"How was the offering this week?"

On and on I went, then all of the sudden I noticed that he was standing awkwardly close to my right shoulder. I looked up at him and at that moment he stuck a white opened envelope near the tip of my oversized, crooked, beautiful nose. And he said these profound Lead Pastor words of divine wisdom to me, "Dude, I haven't heard a word you said."

I said, "What?" He said, "Look at this...You're not going to believe it!"

I stood up opened the envelope and inside it contained a note that read, *"Please use this for whatever the church may need."* —Anonymous.

Wrapped up in that small handwritten note was a cashier's check with no address, no name, written to our church for $130,000. I looked at him, and within about a forty-five-second time span, we jumped up and down like little kids, we high-fived, we hugged, we shouted, we laughed, we cried, and then we sat down in awe and amazement.

(I still get chills about this moment as I type these words.) It was incredible!

Then he said, "Jimmy, What are we going to do?"

I said. "Get the bags ready, this is just the beginning. I believe God has even greater things in store for our church."

I led us in prayer, I just had to praise God for what He had done. I said, "God. Thank you for this check. Lord, we believe that with You, all things are possible. Help us to use every penny for the upbuilding of Your kingdom through Now Church. We know this is just the beginning. May we see many souls saved, many people baptized, relationships mended, families focused and on fire for You. In Jesus Name, Amen!"

If you have any doubts that God can do anything, I can promise you He can!

In fact, I can give you 130,000 reasons why you should believe with every fiber of your being that God can do anything. Our faith in God always makes an investment in the blessings of heaven! Grace reaches down. Faith reaches up. I have had many people ask me who I thought gave that check to our church, and my response is always the same. God. We receive every gift that God is handing out by faith.

We Receive Every Gift That God Is Handing Out By Faith

I believe God gave us that check. Now, it seems pretty evident that He used someone to birth that miracle into our church and He continues to provide for us now through different people and resources, but that was the one that really jump-started it all. I pray that your faith in God will continue to increase. Maybe you just prayed the prayer of salvation and have just begun your journey with Jesus. Maybe you've been walking with Jesus for over fifty years. No matter where you are between birth and heaven, I want your faith in God to be increased! You may be walking through a very difficult situation. I want you to know, God can do anything. Grab the bags!

You may be seeing the world from the peaks of victory, I want you to know, God can do anything! Throughout the next five chapters of this book, I am going to share with you what I have discovered in my twenty years of ministry about how easily our faith can waver.

I call them the Five Characteristics of an Unbelieving Heart:

1. Ignoring God's Word.
2. Ignorance of God's Word.
3. Indifference toward God's Word.
4. Independence from God's Word.
5. Insubordination to God's Word.

As you read, you may realize that you struggle with one or some or maybe even all of these characteristics. If that's the case, I want you to know that God can do anything! And I pray that, as you read, the Lord will reveal to you where your faith wavers in Him and you'll begin to allow Him to work in those troubled areas of your mind and soul.

I pray that you will be changed by the power and promises of His Word because as Paul says, "So then faith comes by hearing, and hearing by the word of God" (Rom. 10:17).

8

Talk to the Hand!

In Him you also trusted, after you heard the word of truth, the gospel of your salvation; in whom also, having believed, you were sealed with the Holy Spirit of promise. (Ephesians 1:13)

I was in high school during the '90s, and I am a proud graduate of the class of 1999 from Rittman High School in Rittman, Ohio! In that decade there were tons of culture shaping words and catch phrases.

Whatever! Was one all the girls were saying, with an eyebrow raise and an eye role.

Waaaaazzzupp! Was one all the guys were saying, from a terrible commercial connecting friends with a non-Nazarene beverage!

TV, Hollywood, and pop culture brought us phrases like, "Did I do that?" Remember that one? How annoying was that?

What about? "Keep the change, you filthy animal."

Remember, "Have mercy!"

Now, "Don't have a cow, man!"

I know I have forgotten some but let me focus in on just two more:

The words, "You got mail," meant so much more than getting something from the United States Post Office. You could type out a message on a computer and send it to another computer anywhere that had the internet, thanks to Al Gore of course! We called it an email, and we still do today. In the '90s you weren't cool if you didn't have an AOL instant messenger screen name. Do you still remember yours? Mine was, "fabulous6723." Hit me up! Just kidding!

But without a doubt my least favorite of all the phrases from the '90s had to be this one, "Talk to the hand!"

Nothing seemed to make me cringe like that phrase. It seemed to be in the hallways daily. It was in the library and the cafeteria. *Talk to the hand.* It was so degrading to the person who was trying to communicate to another person.

Can you imagine this scenario? God sends His messenger, Gabriel, to Mary—a young teenage girl—to reveal to her that she will birth the Son of God with the message, "Mary, you are greatly blessed and highly favored, the Lord is with you, and you will give birth to Jesus Christ." And Mary, confused, responding "But how can this be, I've never had sexual relations?"

"With God all things are possible!" Gabriel assures her. And in that moment Mary throws her hand up, looks at Gabriel, and says, "Talk to the hand," does a hair toss, and walks away!

I am so glad Mary didn't ignore the fact that God can do anything. I am so glad she didn't ignore this foundational Christian truth, that with God all things are possible!

Nevertheless, often we ignore His word. We ignore His ways. We ignore His truth. We throw our hands up at the fact that God can do anything, and tell the creator of all the universe to talk to the hand. How dare we ignore the truth spoken to us! Many sit in churches week after week, or watch an online service and God speaks to their hearts, and they ignore what He is telling them. It's impossible for faith to reach up when you're ignoring God's Word.

Just because we ignore Luke 1:37, doesn't change the fact that it is true. God can do anything. To ignore someone, something, or even God, takes willpower. It takes effort.

When we ignore the Word of God, we express to Him that we are fine with where we are in life. We're good. When we ignore that God can do anything, we demonstrate our belief that we don't need Him in our lives.

We throw up our hand, we toss our hair, and we walk away. Ignoring God expresses to Him that we don't need His help. How could anyone ignore God's promises, His Word, His warnings, His grace, His mercy, His love? Why would anyone allow unbelief to stand between them and the blessings of God? Unfortunately, we do exactly that all the time.

In Hebrews 3 we find a recap of the story of the children of Israel struggling in the desert. We find them wandering, because they had ignored the word of God. Their hearts of unbelief, led them to ignore God's word, and the consequences were incredible. Verse 12 says, "Beware, brethren, lest there be in any of you an evil heart of unbelief in departing from the living God." The people of Israel did not believe that God would give them the victory in Canaan.

They had seen all the plagues that fell on Egypt, they had witnessed God parting the waters of the Red Sea, but they didn't believe that God could win this time. They ignored the fact that God could do anything. That unbelief led to a heart made of stone, and an unbelieving heart is a heart that ignores the word of God. Like the people of Israel, many times we ignore the words of God and miss out on His blessings for our lives and our children's lives. God can do anything.

In what areas of your life are you ignoring that truth?

I can promise you if my beautiful bride Angela looks at me and says, "I love you." I will not ignore that. I won't delay. I won't try to overthink why she loves me, or wonder how could she love me, I will simply respond right back with, "I love you."

God speaks to our hearts, minds, and souls and we should never ignore Him.

He speaks warnings to keep us from harm. He speaks words of comfort and peace. Why would we ignore that?

God really can do anything in your ministry. God can do anything in your home. God really can save anyone, anytime, anywhere. God can do anything. That person you have given up on is the one God specializes in. The one you're praying for might be ignoring God now but that doesn't mean God is ignoring them.

That Person You Have Given Up On Is The One God Specializes In

For fifteen years I prayed for my father-in-law to give his life to Jesus Christ. We would get together, and I would share the love of Jesus with him. We would talk and he would ask questions, and my wife and I would invite him to join us for church, yet someway he would wiggle his way out of attending. In fifteen years I saw him in church two times.

In 2021, out of the blue, he attended a service at our church, another, and then another. Then, during an invitation at our service he gave his life to Jesus Christ and on Christmas Eve 2021, I had the privilege of baptizing him. It was truly a miracle. Fifteen years of prayers, discussions, and heartache finally resolved with the grace found in the glorious gospel of Jesus Christ. He recently shared a story with my wife and said, "I was anxious and worried about a situation. So I just began to pray." He said, "Just three hours later I got a phone call, and my prayers were answered." Then he paused and said, "I guess this stuff does work!" We tried to explain to him prayer doesn't always work that fast, but it always works.

Don't give up. Don't stop praying, don't stop believing that with God all things are possible. Don't ignore His promises. God is moving. God is working. God is speaking. Don't ignore this truth found in the Word of God.

Many continue to live their lives ignoring the Word of God. They may see it on a social media post but ignore it. They may encounter it in a sermon, but they ignore it. They may even have a copy of the Bible, but they ignore it. They ignore what the Bible says, ignore how the creation all around them is declaring the glory of God.

The Book of Malachi is found right before the New Testament begins. It's the last book of the Old Testament and describes events that happened about 400 years before the conversation between Gabriel and Mary about the miraculous birth of Jesus Christ. Malachi's name means, "God's Messenger," it means, "One who carries the Word of God."

The people were questioning God's Word; they doubted it. They continued to break His laws over several thousand years of disobedience, and they continued to ignore almost all of the prophets in the Old Testament. After a series of questions that centered on, "How have we ignored You?" Then they ask in Chapter 3 verse 7, "In what way shall we return?"

The book ends by summarizing the entire Old Testament and a call to remember, don't ignore the law of Moses, and the word of God a thousand years before.

Do you see the common theme running throughout Scripture? Don't ignore the Word of God; take note of the Word of God, do not ignore it.

God can do anything. Don't ignore that today. He doesn't want you to live this life on your own, stumbling along trying to survive. He wants you to trust Him, He wants you to believe His word. Don't ignore the fact that God can do anything.

God makes this statement in Malachi 3, "For I am the Lord, I do not change; Therefore you are not consumed, O sons of Jacob" (Mal. 3:6). If He didn't want the people to ignore His word in the Old Testament, and He didn't want people to ignore His word in the New Testament, then we can be certain, He doesn't want us ignoring His word today. Let's look at another Old Testament story.

In First Samuel 15 we find the story of King Saul in time of war being surrounded with a difficult situation. We can be sure that when we ignore any of God's Word, we will find ourselves in difficult situations without God's help. The Amalekite nation was wicked. They did not fear God and terrorized the nation of Israel for 300 years. God had given them opportunities, yet they refused to turn their hearts toward Him.

They wouldn't look in God's direction, and they continued to bring great harm to His people. God's word had been spoken to King Saul through Samuel with very specific instructions to destroy all the people and all the things of the Amalekite nation. So Saul listened to the Word of God spoken through Samuel...well almost. He kinda listened to Samuel, but he ignored some of God's word, well most of it, well pretty much all of it. He kills some Amalekites, he lets some get away, he takes some prisoners, he takes some sheep, some ox, and some other good stuff.

Samuel confronts King Saul about the situation and Saul found himself in a tough spot, because Saul knew when God told someone to do something, He expected them to obey and not ignore any part of His command. Saul is quick to give an excuse for his actions in verse 15 of the chapter when he says, "They have brought them from the Amalekites; for the people spared the best of the sheep and the oxen, to sacrifice to the Lord your God; and the rest we have utterly destroyed" (1 Sam. 15:15).

There's a couple things I want you to notice. First, King Saul says, "We kept the best for a sacrifice to God." This is important, because many times when people ignore the word of God and are faced with the consequences of their actions they try to make "Holy Excuses."

Our good intentions do not cover up us ignoring what God's Word says. The next and maybe most sad part of this statement is when King Saul says, "A sacrifice to the Lord your God." Did you notice that? He says, "your God," not "my God." Most of the time, actions speak louder than words, but in this case, and in the case of all non-believers, King Saul doesn't even claim God as his God. That's why he ignored His word to begin with, because God was not his God. Saul was Saul's god.

The Lord was not Saul's Lord; Saul was his own lord. In Saul's mind there was only one king in Israel and it was Saul. God makes it clear throughout all of His Word that He calls people, informs people, speaks to people, that He fully expects us to listen and obey His Word that has been given to us. When

God tells us what He wants us to do, or not do, He expects obedience from us.

When God Tells Us What He Wants Us to Do or Not to Do He Expects Obedience from Us

How are you ignoring God?

Are you ignoring Him in your personal life?

Are you ignoring Him in your relationships?

Are you ignoring Him in your ministry, your staff position, your church?

Do not ignore God's Word! Do not ignore the fact that God can do anything!

9

Two Ears...One Mouth.

But He said, "More than that, blessed are
those who hear the word of God and keep it!"
(Luke 11:28)

I'll never forget when my son Hutson was four
years old and we were driving on a beautiful
warm summer day. We had grabbed some ice cream,
and we put the sunroof down, and Hutson was in
the back seat just talking up a storm—on and on he

went—he was talking about his ice cream, he was talking about baseball, and he was talking about his sandals. Talk, talk, talk, he just kept talking. Angela and I were in the front seat, and we looked at each other with amazement.

Finally, I interrupted his talking and said, "Hutson, what in the world are you going on about?"

He grinned and gave us a cute giggle and said, "I'm just going on!"

Now, he comes from a long line of great talkers. My mom was a musician and she taught vocal lessons for many years. When I was young, she would put me on "voice rest," which I assumed helped me at the time, but looking back on it now, I'm pretty sure she just wanted me to shut up.

She also would say this, "God gave you two ears and one mouth, so you should listen twice as much as you talk!"

I sure wish I could say I have mastered that, but I haven't. I don't believe that God speaks to us as much as we think He does. However, I also know He speaks to us more than some people realize. He speaks through His Word. He speaks through His Gospel. He speaks through His Holy Spirit, and He speaks to us through His creation.

Are we listening?

God Doesn't Speak to Us as Much as We Think He Does, But He Speaks to Us More Than We Realize

In fact, David the King writes about this in Psalm 19 when he says, "The heavens declare the glory of God, And the firmament shows His handiwork. Day unto day utters speech, And night unto night reveals knowledge. There is no speech nor language where their voice is not heard" (Ps.19:1–3).

Back in 2009, my friend and mentor, Dr. Dan DeHass, asked me to go with him to Virginia Beach, Virginia, for a three-day revival. Once we loaded the vehicle and headed down Interstate 77, he looked over at me and said, "We're going to stop in Lynchburg, Virginia, to meet up with my friend Norm Pratt." Then he says, "He's going to go to Virginia Beach with us."

I don't really like surprises, and traveling with one guy over the age of sixty is always bad enough, but I wasn't sure I could handle two guys over the age of sixty. You know, men over the age of sixty have the gift of turning a four-hour trip into an eight-hour trip, but I sure am glad I didn't miss out on this opportunity, 'cause God was about to use these two men to pour into my life for a long time. I had no idea that for the next three years after this first trip,

I would be blessed to travel with them both all over the country.

We went all over the place spreading the gospel of Jesus Christ. Not just churches, conferences, and revivals, but bookstores, gas stations, rest areas— lots of rest areas, hotels, restaurants. We were taking the Gospel everywhere. It was so much fun, and I learned so much. I always tell people, traveling with Norm and Dan was like earning a four-year degree in ministry. My ministry would have never survived without Norm and Dan's love, support, and mentorship to me over the years.

When we arrived in Lynchburg that first time, we met for dinner with Norm and his lovely wife Linda. After dinner Norm wanted to take us around the campus of Thomas Road Baptist Church and Liberty University. It was absolutely breathtaking; I had never seen a Christian establishment quite like it.

Dan leaned over the back seat and said, "I want to see Dr. Falwell's grave."

We drove to the site, got out of the vehicle, and began to walk to the memorial. Linda and Dan stopped and looked at some beautiful flowers planted near the sidewalk of the memorial and offices. For some reason, Norm and I continued to talk and walk while we were headed to the memorial and separated ourselves from them.

As we leaned on the fence and looked down at the grave, Norm began to weep. I didn't say a word. We just stood there in the moment. Then he began to point across the mountainside, and said, "Do you see that building?"

I said, "Yes."

He said, "Do you see that building?"

I said, "Yes."

He continued, "Do you see that complex? Do you see that field? Do you see those dorms?"

I said, "Yes," to each of them.

He then said, "All of what you see here is because this man believed that God can do anything." When he spoke those words to me, the world seemed to go silent, and what seemed like forever was just a few moments, but I could hear the Spirit of God speaking to my heart asking me, *Do you believe I can do anything?*

That moment changed me. Right there on that mountain over the grave of a man who I had never met in my life, God had spoken to me. Norm's words changed me. That moment changed my ministry and my entire outlook on life. I was speechless, but my spiritual ears were working great. I could clearly hear what God was speaking to my heart, mind, and soul. I really do believe God can do anything. In that moment God was speaking, and I am so glad I didn't miss it.

You see, God is always speaking. He was speaking to you in the past. He is speaking to you right now. I am so glad that on that mountaintop on the campus of Liberty University overlooking Lynchburg, Virginia, and the Blue Ridge Mountains, God spoke words of life to my soul. I am so glad that I listened to His words in that moment, because if I hadn't, I don't want to even imagine where I would be today.

We are blessed when we listen to the Word of God.

We are happy when we listen to the Word of God.

We will be changed when we listen to the Word of God.

God Is Always Speaking

We should be listening twice as much as we are speaking. There's a lot of truth in that statement. However, I think many people and many believers have that backwards, they talk twice as much as they listen. In 2020 the world was hit with a global pandemic. I never dreamt in a million years that I would be navigating a church through something like we went through. It was such a difficult time for our church, our staff, and our leadership. Daily I had to remind myself and our people that God is in control; God can do anything! For five years we had prayed for a building, and in 2019 God answered our prayers and we received a building. Then in March of 2020, I preached to an empty sanctuary, staring into an iPad.

During that time I poured out my heart to God. I fell on my knees and cried out to Him, and many, many times, I asked "Lord, what is going on?" I remember saying things like, "We need more paper towels. We need more bleach. We need more hand sanitizer, ammo, and of course toilet paper!"

Don't laugh! I bet you stocked up on something too.

I remember spending time in prayer with God, begging Him to protect my family, to protect our church, to protect my friends, and myself. And then suddenly I realized something: I was talking too much.

Have you ever realized you were talking too much and not listening enough? Listening brings wisdom! In fact, Proverbs 1says, "A wise man will hear and increase learning, And a man of understanding will attain wise counsel" (Prov. 1:5).

Have you ever said too much? Have you ever spoken too soon?

We can't hear what God has stored up for us if we don't ever shut up.

We listen with so much more than just our ears, we listen with our hearts, our minds, and our souls. Listening to the Word of God will always affect our actions. My question to you is, what are you going on about? Are you doing all the talking and not listening?

God is speaking. Are you listening?

We hear lots of words of fear being spoken in our world today, but listen to this: Jesus says, fear not. Many fear losing all their money, but listen to this: Jesus says, fear not. Many fear their health may be failing, but listen to this: Jesus says, fear not. Jesus says, fear not!

Did you know that there are about 800,000 words recorded in Scripture? That's a lot of words. Each word is just as vital as the others. Each word connects with the others. The Bible is filled with words of wonder, words of inspiration, words of hope. It's filled with words of wrath, peace, victory, and defeat. Each and every word was chosen and inspired by God to speak to all of mankind as if God is speaking directly to each of us. We should be listening. I believe God is speaking to us today! He is not silent. His words echo loud and clear.

If God Is Speaking, We Should Be Listening

Hebrews 1 says, "God, who at various times and in various ways spoke in time past to the fathers by the prophets, has in these last days spoken to us by His Son, whom He has appointed heir of all things, through whom also He made the worlds" (Heb. 1:1–2).

As we hear the Word of God we must listen to the Word of God.

He has a better word for us than the world has to offer. God's Word covers a wide variety of topics. We should listen to what His Word has to say. Its pages contain the origin of man, the cosmic universe, and all of creation. It contains some, not all but some, of the majestic, mysterious, divine nature of God Himself. It unveils man's sinful nature and his redemption.

The Bible has literally transformed the lives of millions of people. It has motivated them to be missionaries, ministers, and martyrs. It has helped them to become better spouses, better parents, better friends, better neighbors, better employees, and better bosses. In Psalm 19 David puts it this way, "The law of the Lord is perfect, converting the soul; The testimony of the Lord is sure, making wise the simple" (Ps. 19:7). The Word of God must not be ignored. We must not be ignorant to what it says! God can do anything!

Are you feeling lost today? God's Word says in John 14, "Jesus said to him, I am the way, the truth, and the life. No one comes to the Father except through Me" (John 14:6). Jesus invites you to trust Him. Look to Him. Listen to Him. Live for Him.

Do you find yourself worrying? God's Word says in Matthew 6, "Look at the birds of the air, for they neither sow nor reap nor gather into barns, yet your heavenly Father feeds them. Are you not of more value than they?" (Matt. 6:26).

Jesus begs us not to worry, because He knows we have a heavenly Father who will always take care of us!

Are you wrestling with fear and anxiety? God's Word says in Joshua 1, "Have I not commanded you? Be strong and of good courage, do not be afraid, nor be dismayed, for the Lord your God is with you wherever you go" (Josh. 1:9).

The Lord expresses the battle belongs to Him, and we are victorious through our Savior Jesus Christ.

Do you feel surrounded? God's Word says in Psalm 91, "I will say of the Lord, 'He is my refuge and my fortress; My God, in Him I will trust'" (Ps. 91:2).

The Word of God is awesome! It is powerful. It is true. I wish I could give you a thousand more verses but I won't; however, I will give you one more.

I saved one of my favorites for last.

Do you want to prosper and be successful? By the way I have never asked that question and heard someone say, "No, no thanks, I want to be a real loser!" I don't believe anything inside of us says, *Hey! I think I'll be a loser when I grow up!*

It's just not the case. It's not who we are. It's not who God has created us to be!

Oh shoot, I've gotta add one more verse in here. Sorry!

Ecclesiastes 3 says, "He has made everything beautiful in its time. Also, He has put eternity into man's heart" (Eccl. 3:11). God makes it clear to us all that He has placed eternity in all our hearts, and it's His desire to create something beautiful in our lives. What a promise!

Okay, back to one of my favorite verses. There's a driving force inside of us that wants to be successful that wants to prosper. Did you know God has a game-plan for that very thing in His Word? It's found in Joshua 1 and it says this, "This Book of the law shall not depart from your mouth, but you shall meditate on it day and night, so that you may be careful to do according to all that is written in it. For then you will make your way prosperous, and then you will have good success" (Josh. 1:8).

Do see the importance of hearing, reading, studying, and knowing the Word of God?

It's vital we know the Word of God, so we recognize the voice of God.

For us not to be ignorant of the Word of God we must read it! Tape it on our fridge. Listen to it! Make a note to read it, set a reminder to read it every single day! Study it! Re-read it! Study it some more. Know it! We must listen to and learn the words of God found in the Bible! It will increase our faith and open the promises of heaven!

10

It Is What It Is

For whatever is born of God overcomes the world.
And this is the victory that has overcome the
world—our faith. Who is he who overcomes the
world, but he who believes that Jesus is the Son of
God? (1 John 5:4–5)

For those of you who didn't grow up in northeast Ohio, let me share a little secret with you,
we love the two "Bs!" We may love them a little
too much, some would say we're a little over the
top, some would say we're fanatics and that may
be true. But we love our Cleveland Browns and our

Ohio State Buckeyes! Browns and Buckeyes! "Here we go Brownies! Here we go! WOOF! WOOF!" And "O-H-I-O!" Is our love language! I mean you just don't have a choice, before the foundations of the world were established, you were destined to cheer for the Browns and Buckeyes if you were born in northeast Ohio. Just teasing, some of you just threw the book across the room.

We cry when they win, and we cry when they lose!

It was April 23, 2005, and the first day of the NFL Draft. Draft day is like the Super Bowl for us as Browns fans, in fact they made a movie about it, in case you didn't know.

I don't endorse it, just wanted you to know how big of a deal draft day is.

That year we had a Top 10 pick, and there was a long list of some outstanding players who could really help our team. The pick was in, and the announcement was made, we drafted a wide receiver from the University of...What? Where? Why? No! Not the team up north! Anywhere but there! Okay, breathe... just breathe. Now he was a member of the Cleveland Browns. Now he was a part of our team. We can overlook his college choice. Plus, he was big, really big. He was fast, really fast, and all the broadcasters boasted of his great hands.

So even though he was from the school up north, I was willing to overlook it, I was willing to give him a chance to help my Browns. I was certain he was going to lead the league in catches, receiving yards, yards after catch, and of course touchdowns.

And then the season started, but he began the season injured. He eventually played a few games and then got injured again.

In 2007 he had an outstanding year and things were looking up but then 2008 came and things took a terrible twist in that season. And that year he led the NFL...in dropped passes!

In a locker room post-game interview, the media asked him a very simple question: "What's up with all the drops?" I fully expected some great excuse, something like, "It's so cold in Cleveland." Or "These gloves aren't as sticky as the one's I wore in college." Or "I just can't seem to focus because all I can think about is how much money I am making."

I think all of these would have been great excuses, and I would have gladly accepted those as I watched in my pj's under my buffalo plaid blanket. But his response really got to me, in fact, I have never forgotten it. He looked right into the camera and said these words, "It is what it is."

That was it! The camera cut back to the reporter and that was it. I couldn't believe it.

"It is what it is!" That was the first time I had ever heard anyone say that, and I was incredibly upset about it. Unfortunately now it has become a very common saying. The indifference displayed in this statement is absolutely terrifying, especially if made concerning the Word of God. I fear many have become indifferent to the Word of God.

Can you imagine if Mary would have said, "Well, it is what it is," to Gabriel when the angel told her God can do anything. But how often do we do this when we read or hear the Word of God? Many times we are indifferent to the Word of God. Just because we don't care what the Word of God says doesn't change the fact that with God all things are possible. God can do anything! An attitude of apathy should not be our response to the Word of God.

An Attitude Of Apathy Should Not Be Our Response To The Word of God

The Word of God should ignite our souls; it should give us burning hearts and eyes focused on His Word.

Jesus warns of being indifferent when He addresses the Laodicean church; He calls it being "lukewarm," half in, or maybe half out, just a little faith but not too much. Jesus makes it clear that lukewarm Christians make Him sick to His stomach. He makes it clear to us all that He would rather have us, "hot or cold," and that there is no halfway, kinda, sorta when believing His Word.

There is no gray area here when following Jesus Christ. You can't be kind of saved. You're either living for Jesus or living for the devil. You're either on the narrow path or the wide path. You are either light or you are darkness; there is no such thing as dimly lit. You are either hot or cold. Unfortunately, many times we are indifferent to the Word of God. Just because we don't care what the Word of God says doesn't change the fact that with God all things are possible! We should never sigh or roll our eyes at the Word of God.

We Should Never Sigh or Roll Our Eyes At The Word Of God

We should never shrug our shoulders at God's Word. It is true. It's God's grace reaching down to us, and we should embrace it by faith.

I think as believers, followers, and disciples of Jesus Christ we often forget that there is no other book like the Bible! No other book has changed lives like the Bible. No other book offers hope to a hopeless world like the Bible does. No other book tells a story of redemption like the Bible.

I love my Bible. In fact, I cherish my Bible so much, when I travel, I double and triple check to make sure I haven't left it in a hotel room. I have many copies of the Bible and in many different versions, but my favorite is one that was given to me as a high school graduation present from a pastor friend.

I love that Bible, it's highlighted in spots, underlined, circled, and I've written small notes all throughout it. You see, I love my Bible because I believe that it is truly the Word of God, given to us as a gift from God Himself. It is a love letter written from the realms of glory to us here on this earth. Since the completion, it has made an impact on the lives of those who truly read it and believe it. The Bible has a unique way of changing the hearts and minds of those who hear and learn from its words past and present.

The Word of God Is Given to Us as a Gift from God Himself

In fact the Bible has made an impact on some of the greatest minds in our recent history. Look at what some very prestigious people have said about the Bible. Abraham Lincoln, the sixteenth President of the United States of America, said this about the Bible, "I believe the Bible is the best gift God has ever given to man. All the good from the Savior of the world is communicated to us through this book."

Dwight Eisenhower, the thirty-fourth President of the United States said this, "The Bible is endorsed by the ages. Our civilization is built upon its words. In no other book is there such a collection of inspired wisdom, reality, and hope."

The incredible novelist Charles Dickens said this, "The New Testament is the very best book that ever was or will be known in the world."

And maybe my favorite of all of the quotes about the Bible came from Ronald Regan, a famous Hollywood actor who ended up being the President of the United States, who said this about the Bible, "Within the covers of the Bible are the answers for all the problems men face." If only we would read it and believe it.

I am not ashamed to proclaim to you that I believe the Bible. I confess my own faith in the Bible. I believe it is the word of God. I believe it to be true from cover to cover. I believe it is a map for our journey of life and a methodology by which we are to live our lives. I believe it is vital to all believers that we read it, study it, believe it, and apply it to our daily lives.

The Word of God was written down by men and recorded by men but it was inspired by the Spirit of God. In fact, the Bible declares its own authenticity through the Apostle Paul as he writes these words to young Timothy, "All Scripture is given by inspiration of God, and is profitable for doctrine, for reproof, for correction, for instruction in righteousness, that the man of God may be complete, thoroughly equipped for every good work" (2 Tim. 3:16–17).

I love Paul's use of the word, *All*. Did you notice how it jumpstarts that verse? All Scripture, not some of it, but all of it, has been given by inspiration of God Himself.

God inspired men through His Holy Spirit, which is vital. Without this inspiration we have just another book, but with it, we have the Word of God. Like the unity found in the Holy Trinity: God the Father, God the Son, God the Holy Spirit, we see it on every page of the Bible.

The Bible is a collection of 66 books written over a period of 1,600 years. A span of 40 generations, and written by an estimated 40 different authors from every imaginable walk of life.

Let me give you a few. Let's start with Moses. He was a political leader, trained in the Egyptian educational system. Peter was a fishermen. Amos was a sheep farmer. David was a giant slayer. Joshua was a military general. Solomon was a wise king. Nehemiah was a cup bearer to check for poison for the protection of the king. Daniel was a prime minister. Luke was a doctor. Matthew was a tax collector. Paul was a tentmaker and scholar.

And yet, with all these different writers, the message stayed the same, it remains united and crystal clear: God's grace is reaching down to all mankind.

Not only was the Bible written by many different authors from many different areas of life, but they were from all different areas of the world. Portions of the Bible were written in a wilderness. Some parts were written in a dungeon, some on a hillside or in a cave, and others in a palace.

Paul wrote a majority of his portion in Roman prisons, while Luke would write as he traveled, and

John wrote in exile on a deserted island. Some of the Bible was even written from a battlefield under the intense pressures of war. David wrote in times of war; Solomon wrote in times of peace. Some writings came in great times of joy and celebration and others from the depths of despair and sorrow.

The Bible was even written across global divides. It was written on three different continents: Asia, Africa, and Europe. There are no borders to a God who can do anything. The Bible was also written in three different languages, Hebrew, Aramaic, and Greek. Yet under all the different types of circumstances, and communications from all different places and people, the message remained unified and clear to the readers. It is the message of God's grace on full display, covering all of time and all of mankind.

Even though the Bible was written in different places, by different people dealing with different circumstances of life, it was penned, protected, and preserved all these years for us to read it and believe it. There's many reasons why we should read the Bible and believe it; why we should study the Bible and mediate on its words daily. The benefits are far greater than we could ever dream or imagine.

Our world is starving spiritually from a lack of the Word of God.

Our World Is Starving from a Lack of the Word of God

Recently we had a family visit our church. They had been Catholic for over fifty years. That Sunday, as I got up to preach, I said, "Take out your Bible, on your phone, tablet, or whatever device you are using and turn with me to Matthew 25:14–30." And for some reason, I asked them to stand together as I read the Word of God.

Now, I don't do this every week, but I do occasionally, and that Sunday I felt led by the Spirit to do so, and I did. After the service I met with the family, we set up a time for dinner, and later my wife and I took them out for dinner.

As we began talking, the man said to me, "You know, we've attended Catholic Mass faithfully for fifty years, and our priest never once told us to look at our Bible. That really impacted us when you said that on that Sunday and made us stand together to read it."

Since then, the entire family has been saved and baptized in our church. They actively serve in different areas of ministry, and their son is hoping to attend a Christian university when he graduates high school. Why? I believe it's because of the power of the Word of God.

Our awesome vocalist wasn't what they needed to hear that morning. My incredible communication skill wasn't what they needed to hear. Our amazing church announcements weren't what they needed to hear. They needed to hear the Word of God. Proverbs 4 says, "My son, give attention to my words; Incline your ear to my sayings. Do not let them depart from your eyes; Keep them in the midst of your heart; For they are life to those who find them, And health to all their flesh" (Prov. 4:20–22).

The Word of God Brings Life

Our world needs the Word of God. You and I need the Word of God. Our families need the Word of God. Our churches need the Word of God. We must never have a ho-hum attitude toward the Word of God. We must never take it for granted, and allow it to go in one ear and right out the other. We must believe it, live it, preach it, and teach it.

I believe God can do all things; we should never roll our eyes at that glorious statement.

11

I Got This.

Above all, taking the shield of faith with which
you will be able to quench all the fiery darts of the
wicked one." (Ephesians 6:16)

Tucked away toward the end of the Bible is a
little book written by a man named James. I
was named after him; the Book of James was one of
my parents favorite books in the Bible.

James never specifically identifies exactly who
he is in his book but it is commonly accredited to

James, who was the half-brother of Jesus. Can you imagine being the brother of Jesus? I can't imagine how difficult that would have been. Think of all the problems that would have created at dinner discussions and holidays!

You think your family has stress, expectations, and a good name to uphold? Imagine the family of Jesus. James had to play hide-and-seek with Jesus! Think how much fun that would have been: "97–98–99–100! Ready or not . . .." " I found you! My turn to hide!" Kinda fun to think about, isn't it?

"Alright, Jesus! Let's race to that tree. On your mark: Ready, Set, Go!" Then there's Jesus standing there smiling, waiting for him at the tree! You get the point. It would have been tough being the brother of Jesus. It would have given James perfect conditions to envy his brother, maybe even despise him.

The Bible gives some insight on James. He wasn't a believer of Jesus during His time on earth. We find this in Mark 3:21–35 and in John 7:5. Thankfully, eventually James became a believer! After Jesus resurrects and talks with his brother, James changes his perspective on all of the things Jesus did and said, and James became one of the greatest leaders of the early church in Jerusalem.

James proclaimed the gospel of Jesus Christ up until his death and was even labeled by the Apostle Paul as a pillar of the faith in Galatians 2, "and when James, Cephas, and John, who seemed to be pillars, perceived the grace that had been given to me, they gave me and Barnabas the right hand of fellowship, that we should go to the Gentiles and they to the circumcised" (Gal. 2:9).

The Book of James opens with these words, "James, a bondservant of God and of the Lord Jesus Christ, To the twelve tribes which are scattered abroad: Greetings" (James 1:1).

Did you catch that? He could have opened his book up with, "James, the brother of Jesus!" Honestly, I bet most of us would have started it that way, but James didn't. He wanted to be clear that he was a humble servant of God! The language that James uses is written with all humility; there's no pride whatsoever. In fact, he calls out the prideful especially in James 4, where we read his frustration with the prideful. James makes it clear that pride is the enemy of the servant of God.

Pride Is the Enemy of the Servant of God

Even the letter at the center of the word of *P-R-I-D-E* is *I*. That's what makes the word so derogatory.

Can you imagine if Mary would have said, "I got this..." when Gabriel told her God can do anything! Imagine her responding with "I can handle it; I don't need your advice. Get out of my business."

When we look at God and say, "I got this," we display our prideful ways. We flick our finger at God. And, obviously, God says He hates this type of attitude. How often do we do this when we read or hear the Word of God? Many times we are too independent for the Word of God. Just because we think we can handle things all on our own doesn't change the fact that we will eventually face things that we can't handle.

If you are like me, this is how a lot of my conversations in praise go with God, "Um, Lord, I didn't realize you could do all things, why didn't you tell me earlier?"

And God usually responds with, "You focus too much on your own abilities and not me."

Many times we want to do things on our own; we don't need the help from God. We allow P-R-I-D-E to get in the way of asking God to provide and do the impossible! It's as if we think things are just too big for God to handle.

Many Times We Allow Pride To Get In The Way Of Asking God To Provide And Do The Impossible

In Acts 17 the brightest minds and deepest thinkers in all of Athens had not discovered the true God or learned of His character. Yet it's more than likely they would have been considered the most intelligent in maybe all the world. But, instead of them being wise, they were ignorant. There is a difference between wisdom and knowledge. Knowledge comes from a classroom; wisdom comes from God.

Knowledge Comes from a Classroom, Wisdom Comes from God

Knowledge is limited. It's earthly and has its source in the systems of the world. Wisdom is unlimited and spiritual in nature. The Apostle Paul points out the folly and foolishness of idolatry, He describes God in creation, he tells us it is God who has put the life cycles in place and set things in order and He has done this throughout all of time. It is God who created man and placed him on earth and Paul makes clear the incredible truth that those who diligently search for God, those who truly desire to know God, those who make a move toward God will find God. God is not far from us, He is not "unknown." Paul shows us that God had given each nation, including Greece, the opportunity to know Him and make a move toward Him. Paul then makes this statement in verse 30, "Truly, these times of ignorance God over-looked, but now commands all men everywhere to repent" (Acts 17:30).

Paul's message remains the same to us today, but the way we must do it to move our focus from me to God. We must never think we are smarter than God. We must lay our pride aside and trust in God.

We Must Lay Our Pride Aside And Trust In God

The message is clear. Everyone, everywhere must repent and believe in Jesus Christ. No matter how intelligent, no matter their social status, no matter what their salary may be. We live in a world that doesn't like to think about God. We live in a world that does not believe in God. We live in a world that does not glorify God. We live in a world striving for more and more. We live in a world full of people who love their toys. As believers of Jesus Christ and His message of redemption, we must show them they need to move from self-reliance to God reliance.

We must teach the importance of being God conscious and God centered instead of self-conscious and self-centered. There is a God and it's not you, and He is not unknown. He is not playing a massive game of hide-and-seek with us. He is not a figment of our imaginations like a pig with wings, like Bigfoot, the Loch Ness monster, or a unicorn. He really does exist. The problem is we're not giving credit where credit is due. We can't move toward God until we realize we are not God.

There is a major difference between us and God. That seems obvious and pretty simple to understand, the distinction should be clear, but do we live like that? Or do we live like we are in control, like we know it all?

There Is A God And It's Not You

John C. Maxwell describes pride like this, *"When you are full of pride on the inside, it makes you stiff, stubborn, and creates strife with others."*

Pride has a way of making us upset when we are told we're making a mistake. A prideful heart is not a learning heart. I want to be an ever-learner. One my favorite questions to ask during staff interviews is: "Are you willing to learn something new?"

Pride has a way of enjoying praise over things we never had control over in the first place. Jesus told us too, love God and love others. It's really hard to do that when our hearts are filled with pride. Our pride competes with other people instead of loving other people, and our pride competes with God instead of loving God. Pride doesn't necessarily want more; it just wants more than someone else.

Back to James, the servant of Jesus, we can learn a lot from James. He says in James 4, "But He gives more grace. Therefore He says: 'God resists the proud, But gives grace to the humble'" (James 4:6).

God gives more grace. God has plenty of grace and He is ready to distribute it to us, but He won't when our pride gets in the way. Pride clogs the pipe of God's grace every single time. But a humble heart and a hand reaching out in faith receives the grace of God over and over again.

God resists the proud, He rejects them, but to those who are humble He gives grace. Faith in God has no pride in self. Faith reaches up; pride looks for answers all around and within.

James then says this, "Draw near to God and He will draw near to you. Cleanse your hands, you sinners; and purify your hearts, you double-minded" (James 4:8).

It is impossible to do that when our lives are driven by pride. If we take a step in His direction, God will take two toward us. Unfortunately, I think we all enjoy feeling like we're in charge at some time or another in our lives, which makes humility so important.

Pride Clogs The Pipe Of God's Grace

In verse 10, James says, "Humble yourself in the sight of the Lord and He will lift you up" (James 4:10).

Faith in God is the desire to do the will of God. The grace of God is sufficient for everyone, and no one can be saved apart from the grace of God. But, like water and oil, grace and pride don't mix. God resists the proud. It is not that God merely doesn't help the proud, but God actually lines Himself up in conflict with them. Humble yourself and lay your pride in the dust.

The prideful heart says, "I don't need God or His Word in my life." In Second Kings chapter 2 we have two prophets of the Lord, or "proclaimers of the Word of God," Elijah and Elisha. In this chapter we see them making a final journey together just before Elijah is taken up into heaven.

Their route takes them from Gilgal to Bethel to Jericho to the Jordan River. During this trip Elisha is reminded many times that Elijah will soon be taken away, Elijah confirms that his work will continue through Elisha, and he will be faithful to the call to proclaim the word of the Lord. They reach the Jordan River in verses 7–8 and there Elijah performs his final miracle by parting its waters. So then Elisha asks to become Elijah's "rightful successor," and Elijah tells him the requirements.

One of the requirements is to witness his departure from the earth, as Elisha watches a chariot of fire appears, and Elijah is carried into heaven by a whirlwind. Between verses 12 and 25 in chapter 2 Elisha kicks off his ministry, and it starts with a bang. In these first few days he parts the Jordan, he allows fifty prophets to search for Elijah even though he knew he was gone, he purifies some water from a polluted spring at Jericho, and then in verse 23 we find this strange encounter with some young men.

Grace And Pride Don't Mix

> Then he went up from there to Bethel; and
> as he was going up the road, some youths
> came from the city and mocked him, and said
> to him, "Go up, you baldhead! Go up, you
> baldhead!" So he turned around and looked
> at them, and pronounced a curse on them
> in the name of the Lord. And two female
> bears came out of the woods and mauled
> forty-two of the youths. Then he went from
> there to Mount Carmel, and from there he
> returned to Samaria. (2 Kings 2:23–25)

In the original text the phrase "youths" or "small
boys" in this passage could refer to young men. The
age really isn't important, what is important to note
is they mocked God's prophet, who he represents,
and what he represented, the Word of God.

Apparently, they had heard that Elijah had left
the earth and gone up to heaven and they were
hoping the same for Elisha. They were hoping to
rid their land and their lives of God's chosen and of
God's word.

I know it's harsh; I know this story seems sad. But
this story is a reminder for all of us to take the Word

of God seriously as well as God's chosen messengers. Back in the Book of Leviticus, God expressed to His people what He would do if they refused to listen, obey, and believe His Word, and one of those things would be to have them devoured by wild animals.

This story in 2 Kings is a fulfillment and a judgement upon godless parenting. These kids learned to mock and scoff at the word of God and His prophets from somewhere. And the mocking stemmed from a heart of unbelief heard around the house of their parents. You see, unbelief is just as contagious as belief.

Romans 10 makes this clear to us all, "So then faith comes by hearing, and hearing by the word of God" (Rom. 10:17). We need God in our lives. We need the Word of God in our lives. We should never want it out of our lives or think it is not needed.

Unbelief Is Just As Contagious As Belief

When we read the Word of God, it breeds faith in our soul. It strengthens our faith, so we must make reading the Word of God a priority, we must make hearing the Word of God a priority, and we'd better believe it with a humble heart. We must never think we are too good, or too smart, for the Word of God.

Belief in the Word of God is our only hope as individuals. It's our only hope for our families. It's our only hope for our world. We must take God at His word, trust His word, and it will transform us. We need God's power in our lives, and the best way to obtain this is through knowing His Word.

Too often we think, say, "I can do it, I can do it, I can do it." We should stop and say, "You know what, I can't do it, but I believe God can do all things!" Don't allow pride to stand in the way of the work of our Lord! Don't allow your independence to stand in the way of the miraculous work of God. Want more of God and want more of His Word in your life.

Let's quit pretending like, "We got this," and start believing more and more that God has us in His grace and mercy.

12

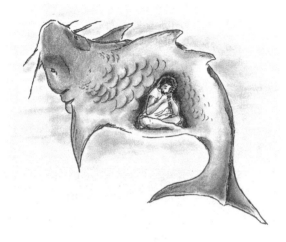

No!

Peter said to Him, "You shall never wash my feet!" Jesus answered him, "If I do not wash you, you have no part with Me." (John 13:8)

Let me tell you a story about Jonah and the _____. Were you able to fill in the blank? I have a feeling you were. The story of Jonah and the whale is quite popular. It's been shared in multiple ways and multiple venues. The story of Jonah is tucked away in the Bible and is often overlooked, or maybe a better word to describe it would be *misunderstood.*

If you think the story of Jonah is about a guy named Jonah it is, but it really isn't. If you think it's just a big fish story it is, but it isn't, even though it does have a worm in the story. The Book of Jonah is a personal account of a man named Jonah who says, "Yes," to God, and says, "No," to God.

There are three basic interpretations of the Book of Jonah.

There's a mythological view. This is a view in which the reader looks at Jonah as one would look upon Greek or Roman mythology.

There's the allegorical interpretation. In this view the book is looked at as an extended parable. Jonah is viewed as Israel. The sea is the gentile nation in general, the fish is Babylonian captivity, and Jonah's release represents the freedom from captivity during Ezra's time.

Then there's the literal-historical interpretation. And this view is ultimately the correct one. The Book of Jonah presents itself as actual history written by Jonah, a prophet of God. The Jews and the Christians in the early church believed it to be literal. Jonah is referred to as a historical person in other in books of the Bible such as Second Kings 14:25 which lists his hometown, the name of his father, and more important than even that is Jesus Christ refers to Him in the gospels while He is on the earth as recorded in Matthew 16 and Luke 11.

The most significant and detailed reference from Jesus of Jonah is found in Matthew 12, which says,

Then some of the scribes and Pharisees answered, saying, "Teacher, we want to see a sign from You." But He answered and said to them, "An evil and adulterous generation seeks after a sign, and no sign will be given to it except the sign of the prophet Jonah. For as Jonah was three days and three nights in the belly of the great fish, so will the Son of Man be three days and three nights in the heart of the earth. The men of Nineveh will rise up in the judgment with this generation and condemn it, because they repented at the preaching of Jonah; and indeed a greater than Jonah is here." (Matthew 12:38–41)

I believe the Bible confirms Jonah was a real person and he was a prophet of God. He was swallowed by a huge fish and his autobiography is pretty incredible. Let's dive into it! (Like what I did there?)

Jonah 1, "Now the word of the Lord came to Jonah the son of Amittai, saying, "Arise, go to Nineveh, that great city, and cry out against it; for their wickedness has come up before Me" (Jon. 1:1–2).

Jonah went to Nineveh, and he obeys God, the end—not quite the way it goes. Verse 3 says, "But Jonah arose to flee to Tarshish from the presence of the Lord. He went down to Joppa, and found a ship going to Tarshish; so he paid the fare, and went down into it, to go with them to Tarshish from the presence of the Lord."

Obey or not obey? Yes or no? God said, "turn left," and Jonah turned right. God said, go east, and Jonah went west. Jonah went to Joppa. He bought a ticket to Tarshish to run from God. Joppa to Nineveh was about 500 miles, however, Joppa to Tarshish was about 2,500 miles away.

Isn't it amazing how far some people will run to try to hide from the presence of God? It can't be done. In fact, King David wrote these words in the Book of Psalms, "If I ascend into heaven, You are there; If I make my bed in hell, behold, You are there" (Ps. 139:8).

Jonah disobeyed God. He rejected God's word.

Many Go Way out of Their Way to Run from God

Rejecting the word of God will bring destruction. The Bible describes Jonah's demise. Jonah went down into Joppa. Jonah went down into the insides of the ship. Jonah went down in the depths of the sea. Jonah went down into the belly of the fish. The same is true with us, a person who rejects God is going down—no matter how successful they may seem, no matter how prosperous they may look— when we reject the Word of God, we head down a path of destruction.

Rejecting the word of God will always have costly consequences. Verse 3 in chapter 1 says, "Jonah paid the fare and went down into it." Notice it didn't say what the price was! But it cost Jonah something. Sin will always cost us something. All throughout the Bible we see the cost of sin.

The Christian is addressed in Galatians 6, "Do not be deceived, God is not mocked; for whatever a man sows, that he will also reap" (Gal. 6:7).

For the lost, for the non-believer, we see the cost of sin described in Romans 6:23, "For the wages of sin is death, but the gift of God is eternal life in Christ Jesus our Lord" (Rom. 6:23).

Sin will always cost something and the pleasures of sin will soon fade away.

Jonah 1says,

Then the mariners were afraid; and every man cried out to his god, and threw the cargo that was in the ship into the sea, to lighten the load. But Jonah had gone down into the lowest parts of the ship, had lain down, and was fast asleep. So the captain came to him, and said to him, "What do you mean, sleeper? Arise, call on your God; perhaps your God will consider us, so that we may not perish." (Jon. 1:5–6)

Sin starts with temptation; it continues with disobedience to God's word. Sin is tempting and it's called temptation for a reason. The enemy doesn't offer heartache, pain, suffering, disease, addiction, death with the first kiss, or the first sip, or the first click, or the first few miles. Be careful in your comfort, soon things will get rocky just like they did for

Jonah, and his sin not only put himself in danger but others as well.

Jonah's sin put others in danger. The pagan pirates were calling out to gods, any god that would hear! But the man of God, the one who God had called was asleep in the bottom of the boat. What a terrifying thought, the man of God, the true believer, was cozy and comfortable while the non-believer's cried out for help to helpless gods. Christians, we must wake up; many are searching for answers in the storms of life.

Christians, We Must Wake Up; Many Are Searching For Answers In The Storms Of Life

They cast lots to see who was to blame on the boat because of the storm and waves, and Jonah wins the prize. The comfort is gone. His rest has ended.

He suggests they throw him overboard, and they do. A monster fish swallows him, and it's here that he comes to a great realization: he's not dead yet, so there's still hope.

Jonah considers his situation. He remembers the God who spoke to him, so he does what only he knows to do, Jonah prays. Jonah 2:1 says, "Then Jonah prayed to the Lord his God from the fish's belly."

The story of Jonah is a story of rejecting, resting, and repentance. Jonah makes this bold proclamation from the depths of His soul in verse 9 of chapter 2, where he says, "But I will sacrifice to You, With the voice of thanksgiving; I will pay what I have vowed. Salvation is of the Lord."

Jonah says, I believe. I will sacrifice my life for you, I will remember Your holy temple. You are the One True God. I praise you. I thank you. I will look in your direction. Jonah prays in his darkest hour, from the darkest depth of the sea and God heard his prayer! If God heard Jonah's prayer, He will hear your prayer. He was a man who said, "No," to God and still survived, in Jonah's life from the belly of a great fish, God's grace reached down and Jonah's faith reached up.

If God Heard Jonah's Prayer, He Will Hear Your Prayer

Verse 10 in chapter 2 says, "So the Lord spoke to the fish, and it vomited Jonah onto dry land." The story of Jonah is a story of rejecting the word of God, resting in the comfort of sin, and repentance; and it's also about God rescuing. God didn't just rescue Jonah to sit on the beach. God rescued him for His original call and spoken word. "Now the word of the Lord came to Jonah the second time, saying, "Arise, go to Nineveh, that great city, and preach to it the message that I tell you" (Jon. 3:1–2).

God Didn't Rescue Jonah To Sit On The Beach

God's plans for Jonah never changed. Even though Jonah disobeyed. He has great plans for you too, but it all starts with obedience to His Word. When we disobey the word of God, we limit the effectiveness and impact of our lives! We obey and serve because we love Him—to serve is to love and there is joy in serving the Lord—and there is joy resting in the fact that God can do anything!

With God all things are possible. Can you imagine if Mary would have said, "No"? I mean flat out looked Gabriel square in the angelic eyes and said, "No!" Mary heard the word of God, she believed and received it. God can do anything. When we abide by this principle of obeying the word of God and apply it to our lives, we release the miracle working power of God into our lives. We can also be certain that our obedience or disobedience to the word of God will always affect our lives and the lives of those around us. Christianity and obedience go hand in hand.

Christianity And Obedience Go Hand In Hand

I usually pray three times during a regular Sunday morning worship service. Once at the beginning, once before I preach, and then to close the service out. At the closing of a Sunday morning worship service, I was praying and I actually put my foot in my mouth spiritually speaking, by the way, it's a pretty big foot I wear size 14 shoes.

In my prayer I said these words in front of our entire congregation,

Lord, I want our church to be so on fire for Jesus Christ, filled so much with the power of Your Holy Spirit that people would drive by this building even when it's empty and feel Your power, feel Your presence, and hear Your voice! Draw people to You. Lord, we lift up the name of Jesus in this place.

And Your word says, "If Jesus be lifted up, that You will draw, men, women and children to You."

Now, I know a majority of this book has been about faith, but can I just be transparent for a moment: in that moment, I lacked faith. I thought to myself, *Man, that was a stupid thing to say.* Did I really believe that was possible? In that moment, on a Sunday morning service, Pastor Jim R. Copenhaver doubted. I had prayed that prayer in my private prayer life, but never in front of our entire congregation.

Weeks and months went by and I had pretty much forgotten about it for the most part and was hoping a majority of my congregation had as well, but I am so glad God hadn't forgotten about it. The Sunday after Easter in 2021, a young lady named Noah walked into our church for the very first time. I preached a sermon titled, "YOLO," from our small talk sermon series, on the reality of we only live once so live it for Jesus Christ. At the end of the service I gave a simple invitation to trust Jesus Christ as Lord and Savior, and in that moment, Noah said, "Yes" to Jesus and was gloriously saved.

After the service she shared her story with some volunteers at our welcome center. On Thursday of that week we had a campus leadership meeting, in the meeting I brought up how cool Noah was and how we needed to connect with her and pray for her in her new relationship with Jesus Christ.

One of the ladies from the welcome center was in our meeting and spoke up and asked, "Do you know her story?" I said, "No." She said, "Well, this is what she told me after church: Noah drives by our church every single day on her way to class at a local college. She said, every day there was something inside of her that told her she had to go to that church. Sunday was her first time in our building. Sunday, she gave her life to Jesus Christ." Her family now attends our church and I have had the privilege of baptizing her and her brother. All because Noah said, "Yes." Grace was reaching down and Noah said, "Yes."

Grace was calling and Noah answered the call. No other god can do this. Grace comes down and empowers faith from the Word igniting a miracle from God. Can you imagine if Mary would have looked up at Gabriel and said, "No"? God's grace always gives our faith an opportunity to respond to Him with a yes! It's God's way of doing business with the entire world. Grace reaches down. Faith reaches up. And miracles happen in between!

13

Pin The Tail
on the False Prophet

Finally, brethren, pray for us, that the word of the
Lord may run swiftly and be glorified, just as it
is with you, and that we may be delivered from
unreasonable and wicked men; for not all have
faith. (2 Thessalonians 3:1–2)

In the Bible we find a crazy story about a man named Balaam who was really torn between being a prophet of the Lord or being a pagan fortune teller. Numbers 22 drops us into the scene where Israel has had some battle victories over the Amorites. Then the Israelites traveled to the plains of Moab and camped along the Jordan across from Jericho. Balak, the Moabite king panicked, because God's people had a reputation of being led by the One True God who could do anything. So Balak decides to call in some reinforcements with this sorcerer named Balaam.

Balaam had a reputation that what he blessed prospered and what he cursed was cursed. He would work for anyone, or any side, it didn't matter to him as long as the check cleared. So King Balak calls on Balaam to curse Israel. Balaam calls on God to find out what he should do. God says. Don't go! Don't do it. Balaam refuses to go. But the king sends more people and promises him more fortune, fame, and honor. Balaam then goes back to God to see what he should do.

Let me show you the text from Numbers 22:

So Balaam rose in the morning, saddled his donkey, and went with the princes of Moab.

Then God's anger was aroused because he went, and the Angel of the Lord took His stand in the way as an adversary against him. And he was riding on his donkey, and his two servants were with him. Now the donkey saw the Angel of the Lord standing in the way with His drawn sword in His hand, and the donkey turned aside out of the way and went into the field. So Balaam struck the donkey to turn her back onto the road. Then the Angel of the Lord stood in a narrow path between the vineyards, with a wall on this side and a wall on that side. And when the donkey saw the Angel of the Lord, she pushed herself against the wall and crushed Balaam's foot against the wall; so he struck her again. Then the Angel of the Lord went further, and stood in a narrow place where there was no way to turn either to the right hand or to the left. And when the donkey saw the Angel of the Lord, she lay down under Balaam; so Balaam's anger was aroused, and he struck the donkey with his staff.

Then the Lord opened the mouth of the donkey, and she said to Balaam, "What have

I done to you, that you have struck me these three times?"

And Balaam said to the donkey, "Because you have abused me. I wish there were a sword in my hand, for now I would kill you!"

So the donkey said to Balaam, "Am I not your donkey on which you have ridden, ever since I became yours, to this day? Was I ever disposed to do this to you?"

And he said, "No."

Then the Lord opened Balaam's eyes, and he saw the Angel of the Lord standing in the way with His drawn sword in His hand; and he bowed his head and fell flat on his face. And the Angel of the Lord said to him, "Why have you struck your donkey these three times? Behold, I have come out to stand against you, because your way is perverse before Me. The donkey saw Me and turned aside from Me these three times. If she had not turned aside from Me, surely, I would also have killed you by now, and let her live."

And Balaam said to the Angel of the Lord, "I have sinned, for I did not know You stood in the way against me. Now therefore, if it displeases You, I will turn back."

Then the Angel of the Lord said to Balaam, "Go with the men, but only the word that I speak to you, that you shall speak." So Balaam went with the princes of Balak.) Num. 22:21–35)

I want to focus on verse 12 in this passage, because here we find the directive will of God is made known to Balaam. It says, "And God said to Balaam, "You shall not go with them; you shall not curse the people, for they are blessed" (Num. 22:12).

And then as the story goes on, in verse 20 we see God gives Balaam permission to go but only speak what He tells him and do what only He tells him.

Balaam was free to go with them, but God had already told him not to go. Sometimes God will let you be wrong once or twice to prove He is always right.

Sometimes God Will Let You Be Wrong Once Or Twice To Prove He Is Always Right

The Bible is referred to as the Word of God, meaning it can be considered a direct line of communication from God Himself and it is interpreted by human authors of each of its respective books.

First Thessalonians says this, "For this reason we also thank God without ceasing, because when you received the word of God which you heard from us, you welcomed it not as the word of men, but as it is in truth, the word of God, which also effectively works in you who believe" (1 Thess. 2:13).

We can't honor the word of God if we don't know what it is and what it says.

Psalm 119 says, "Your word I have hidden in my heart, that I might not sin against You" (Ps. 119:11). The more we desire to know God's Word, the more we will understand God's working and His will in our lives. A recent study done among Christians between 2018 and 2021 were asked the question, "How often do you use the Bible on your own?" Only about 12 percent of people in the survey said they use their Bible daily and unfortunately 29-34 percent said they never read it at all. Our relationship with Christ starts with knowing God's Word.

You can't have a friendship that only communicates in one direction. Without that relationship, we don't have a clue about what God is doing in our lives. It's impossible to know God without knowing God's Word. It's impossible to know God's will for your life apart from His Word. This is how we strengthen our relationship with Him. God was speaking to Balaam.

It amazes me that Balaam talked to God. There is no one we will encounter in this world who God is not dealing with; somehow, someway God is speaking to everyone.

There Is No One We Will Encounter In This World Who God Is Not Speaking To

It's clear that Balaam had some sort of relationship with God, he approached God before he decided to go with Balak's men, and he said, "Hang on. Let me go talk to God first." Do we do that? Do we approach God with the desire to know what He wants to speak over our lives? Or do we just turn up with our wish list?

When we have a relationship with God, we can freely approach the throne and ask for anything. But we need to be wary of how we approach. The Word of God was never meant to just stay in our heads; it was always meant to permeate our hearts.

Sometimes, even though we have a relationship with God, we still mess up and do things for our own gain. Balaam chooses the path of self-will and self-advantage and God did not approve this. Balaam was greedy and God was mad that Balaam went. By His grace, God was stopping his movements. At times

God is angry at what we do. At times God doesn't approve of our actions. At times God doesn't like our plans.

At times God doesn't like the path we are on. Do you ever feel like "everything is against you?" Maybe it is. Maybe it's because God doesn't approve of the direction you are headed. God was trying to help Balaam, so God blocked his direction.

How often is God right in front of us and we miss Him? How many times does He say, "Don't go there; don't do that; don't say that; don't text that; don't look at that"? How many times?

Eventually, God will get your attention, and you will need to make a choice. The choices we make will result in God's grace or God's judgment. They go hand in hand. The grace of God was being shown to Balaam and He missed it.

Lamentations 3 says, "They are new every morning; great is Your faithfulness" (Lam. 3:23).

Romans 6 says, "What shall we say? Shall we continue in sin that grace may abound? (Rom. 6:1).

Acts 17says, "So that they should seek the Lord, in the hope that they might grope for Him and find Him, though He is not far from each one of us" (Acts 17:27).

God is closer than you think. His mercy is working on your behalf. His grace is pointing you in the right direction. Don't miss it. The heavens declare His glory. His grace is amazing and it is nearer than you could dream or imagine. Don't miss it.

Balaam was opposing God's word and was oblivious to it. But look who didn't miss it. Verse 23 says, "Now the donkey saw the Angel of the Lord standing in the way with His drawn sword in His hand, and the donkey turned aside out of the way and went into the field. So Balaam struck the donkey to turn her back onto the road" (Num. 22:13).

The Donkey saw the angel of the Lord, not once, not twice, but three times. Balaam gets mad at the donkey and shouts, "I would kill you if I had a sword on me." Ironically, the angel had a sword drawn ready to kill Balaam at any moment God gave the word.

Balaam never stops to think about the fact that God's grace and judgment are close to Him. When Balaam is confronted by his trusted donkey, and by an angel of the Lord, his response is not one of pride or blame. It is one of regret. But he didn't repent because he was wrong; he was regretting because he got caught.

When God opens our eyes and we realize the awe and majesty of the God we claim to know and serve, we are faced with the reality of how far off we truly are. We have to make a choice. Are we going to get on track, do the things God wants us to do, the things He is speaking to us, like loving our neighbor, serving our community?

Unfortunately, Balaam's spiritual condition did not end with a happy ending. Joshua describes Balaam as practicing divination, being a cult-member (Josh. 13:22). Then, he is even referred to by three different authors as selling his gift to the highest bidder (2 Peter 2:15), thinking He could force God into doing something He wasn't going to do (Jude 1:11), living doctrinally as someone who believed that if he couldn't condemn his enemy, then he would corrupt them (Rev. 2:14). He was frustrated, filthy, and fallen. Because of all of this, he was eventually executed by the Israelite army. Balaam had a choice and he really chose poorly. The word of God always demands a response, whether it's spoken by a donkey or a pastor.

The Word Of God Always Demands A Response Whether It's Spoken By A Donkey Or A Pastor

We have a choice to make. God's grace and God's judgement are closer than you think. We are what we love. I'm a Ford guy. I'm a Chevy guy. I'm a Coach girl. I'm a Pepsi guy. I'm a Coke guy. These are the things we identify with, which define our identity.

As believers of Jesus Christ, our identity should be wrapped up in Christ alone. Believers are sons and daughters of the One True God and possess a divine nature in Christ Jesus. Believers have the Holy Spirit dwelling inside of them. Believers have Christ and Christ has them. Being a believer in Jesus Christ is a big deal! Christ changes everything.

A child of God is the product of God's new creative power in their life at the moment of salvation. The same creative power found all throughout scripture from Genesis to Revelation. We find it in His Holy Spirit, His Gospel, and clearly described in His Word. He can make all things new, because He has made all things. Way too often I fear believers forget who our identity is supposed to be fully in.

I know Christians right now who will fight you over their favorite politician, but their coworkers don't even know they attend church once a month let alone claiming a belief in Jesus Christ. It shouldn't be that way.

There is no secret service in the army of the Lord. It should not be a surprise to the world that we believe that with God all things are possible. We must not ignore His promises made in Scripture. We must not stay silent when He has told us to proclaim His good news to the world.

There Is No Secret Service In The Army Of The Lord

Why are we ashamed to have our identity in Christ? I really believe it comes down to belief. A person who truly believes that God can do anything is easily recognizable. Unfortunately, I feel many have faith in their hearts but few display it in their lives.

Are you really a man or a woman of faith? Do you really believe that God is exactly who He says He is and that He can do what He says He can do? Do you believe the Bible to be the inspired Word of God? Do you believe God can do anything? I know, if you do, it will change your entire outlook on life. It will transform your mind. It will empower your life. It will revive your church. It will breed a much needed vibrancy into your family. God can do anything.

As Christians we can no longer just be people of faith and not allow that faith to change our actions, thoughts, and words. If we believe, it should be evident to all the world, and God will always bless our faith.

As Christians We Can No Longer Just Be People of Faith, We Must Allow That Faith To Change Us

Christians should never try to bottle up their faith, it should spill out on every area of their lives and the lives of those around them. Grace is reaching down; if our faith reaches up, miracles will happen in between. We need faith we are willing to die for, but we also need faith we are willing to live for.

God can do anything. Jeremiah 32 says, "Ah, Lord God! Behold, You have made the heavens and the earth by Your great power and outstretched arm. There is nothing too hard for You" (Jer. 32:17). God can do anything.

Job 42 says, "I know that You can do everything, And that no purpose of Yours can be withheld from You" (Job 42:2). God can do anything.

The way we display God's grace to the world is through our faith in Him. God is dwelling inside of us. He is actively working in our world. He is still seeking and saving the lost through His gospel. He is our provider. God's grace is reaching down to this world. How we live will express whether or not we believe that truth.

The Way We Display God's Grace To The World Is Through Our Faith In Him

Other than God, Jesus Christ, and the Holy Spirit, the most important word found in all of Scripture is the word *believe*. Our belief in God is foundational to our spiritual journey. Faith in God is foundational for all things of life and our entire existence.

Our belief in Jesus Christ brings us into a right relationship with a holy God. Without that belief we stand on our own merit—our own good works and deeds. Our belief in the Holy Spirit enables us to live a life that honors God. Belief in the leading of the Holy Spirit puts us on the paths of righteousness as we follow His leading and His way. You see, belief is vital to all Christians, that's why we are often referred to as "believers."

One night my wife and I were on a romantic date! This was before our son was born, so I took her to an extremely high-class hot wing restaurant in our hometown. We were sitting there having a meal and at a table nearby was an extremely popular pastor in our hometown. He was there with mixed group of about twelve people with teenagers and a few young married couples.

We finished our meal and stood up to leave the restaurant when he yelled out, "Jimmy Copenhaver! Come over here!" I knew this was going to be fun, because only people who knew me as a little kid called me "Jimmy." We began to walk over to the table of strangers and before we got there, the pastor jumped up, shook my hand and gave me a hug.

I introduced him to my wife Angela, and then he turned me and her to the table and said these words that continue to echo in my heart and soul. He said this to these dozen strangers: "Hey guys, this is Jimmy Copenhaver. He is one of the most faithful guys you will ever meet. I am so proud of him and what God is doing in his life and ministry."

Now, to some people this would have been a great introduction—especially to a bunch of people that you have never met—but I must admit in the moment I was shocked. In fact, as I got in our vehicle and drove away, I realized that his words for some reason bugged me. I wondered in my mind, Why didn't he say I was an awesome singer; or a dashingly handsome young man, or a good preacher, or even, a great baseball coach.

The best he could come up with was that I was, "faithful," faithful? That incident was many years ago. Can I tell you that his words mean so much more to me today than they ever did back then? You see, the longer I live the more I realize how awesome it is to have someone call me faithful. There's no greater compliment we can be given than to be called faithful. This is what all believers' identity should be found in: a faith in God, faith in His Word, faith in His One and only Son Jesus Christ.

When someone describes us as a person who truly believes that God can do anything, that is a great category to be placed in! To be labeled as faithful means so much more than I realized then, and I'm glad that I am still faithful today! Think about it.

As Christians, our long-term spiritual goal is to hear God Himself say these words found in Matthew 25: "His lord said to him, 'Well done, good and faithful servant; you have been faithful over a few things, I will make you ruler over many things. Enter into the joy of your lord'" (Matt. 25:23).

I'm glad it doesn't say, "all things." God never requires perfection, just faith in Him, while being faithful in a few things. If it said, "all things," we would be perfect and we wouldn't need a perfect Savior, but it says, "a few things." There's still things I want to accomplish in this life but my greatest achievement will be my faithfulness to the anything is possible God.

I want to be a faithful husband. I want to be a faithful dad. I want to be a faithful pastor, friend, teacher, coach, employee, whatever it is I am privileged to do in this life. But most importantly I want God's grace to be on full display by my life of faith in Him.

Will you join me? Let's truly believe that God can do anything? Grace reaches down. Faith reaches up. Miracles happen in between.

14

My Cup

I have been crucified with Christ; it is no longer I
who live, but Christ lives in me; and the life which
I now live in the flesh I live by faith in the Son
of God, who loved me and gave Himself for me.
(Galatians 2:20)

In 2014 my life was like the lyrics of that vintage
Carpenter's song, "Top of the World:"

I'm on the top of the world lookin' down
on creation
And the only explanation I can find
Is the love that I've found, ever since you've
been around
Your love's put me at the top of the world.

Life was incredible! The sky was bluer than it had ever been. I was working as a Bible teacher at a small Christian school and was also the Varsity Baseball Head Coach, and not just any team either, a national championship team. I was traveling on the weekends with an award-winning gospel music quartet, I was really living a dream.

Yet, I continued to hear a quiet, peaceful voice in my heart instructing me in a path that I never dreamt I would head toward. I continued to wrestle with God about starting a church in Orrville, Ohio. I knew all too well the horror stories of starting a church, and even though I may have been foolish enough to take on the task, there was no way my sweet, lovely wife Angela would be willing to join me on this faith expedition. My discussions with God got so intense, I eventually told Him while in prayer, "If this is really what you want me to do, I'll do it, but You have to tell Angela!"

You see, sometimes we know God has instructed us to do something for Him. Sometimes He has revealed to us things that only we are ready to hear from Him. I had to learn this. When I was younger, I would tell others what they were doing wrong spiritually, or what they needed to change, and they weren't ready to hear it. For years I struggled with this, I knew and know, God can't tell you one thing and tell me something else. God cannot lie. Hebrews 6 says, "That by two immutable things, in which it is impossible for God to lie, we might have strong consolation, who have fled for refuge to lay hold of the hope set before us" (Heb. 6:18).

Discerning what God is speaking and showing you and I is so important and it comes with experience as we walk with Him and trust Him more and more.

Everyone May Not Be Ready To Hear What God Has Told You

Everyone may not be ready to see what God has shown you, and everyone may not be ready to receive what God has given to you.

On May 21, 2014, Angela and I had a scheduled lunch date at a very high-class restaurant, a Subway at a local gas station near the school where I was teaching and coaching. It was delicious by the way.

We had a long conversation and I began to share that God had been speaking to my heart about maybe a new chapter in my life, and I wasn't sure what to do about it. After much stumbling over my words, she asked, "Well, what do you want to do?"

In that moment it was like God shot an arrow at my heart, and I knew I had to strike while the iron was hot. I blurted out, "God wants me to start a church in the school."

I hadn't even considered a building, other than I knew it was supposed to happen in Orrville, Ohio. I had completely forgotten to ask God about a building, but it's good to know He knows our every need before we even ask, or even if we forget to ask.

I thought for sure in that moment she was going to throw her 6-inch tuna melt sub sandwich in my face, but thankfully she didn't. I hate tuna.

She looked up into my eyes and very intently said these words, "If that's what God wants you to do, let's do it, I support you 100 percent."

The rest as they say is history, but more like His-story. God is writing your story. God is writing my story. I am so glad He is. My story is not done, and if you're able to read these words or hear these words, your story is not done either. God can do anything.

It is God who writes our story, it's up to us to share it with the world.

It Is God Who Writes Our Story; We Share It With The World

He has great plans for all of us. It's the same message He declared to the prophet Jeremiah when He said, "For I know the thoughts that I think toward you, says the Lord, thoughts of peace and not of evil, to give you a future and a hope" (Jer. 29:11).

After our lunch Angela dropped me off at the front door of the school. When I walked in the front door, the superintendent was standing in the foyer. He was looking at a table set up for the display of our baseball team's national championship trophy, banners, and photos from our trip throughout the tournament. He congratulated me on our incredible victory, and we talked a little about the program. Then he said the words I will never forget.

He said, "Jim, you're a great teacher and a great coach. I've been thinking though, if you ever need our building to start a church, I want you to know that it would be available to you."

I know you and I have just walked through thirteen chapters of the importance of faith, but I honestly could hardly believe what I was hearing. After that day, in just five short months. We launched Faith Community Church in the Kingsway Christian School in Orrville, Ohio.

Eventually, I resigned from the classroom, singing, and coaching to focus fully on ministry. Things were going pretty well. I loved all my jobs and they were a great source of income for our family, but God made it very clear to me to walk away from those and focus on growing our church, one soul at a time.

It was a roller-coaster ride of faith to say the least. Year after year, the trend was not going in the right direction at all. We weren't growing, we weren't any closer to having our own building, our finances were diminishing quickly, and my dynamic preaching and dashing good looks grew our church from fifty people to thirty people.

It was the beginning of a brand-new year, January 2019. While all of you were making New Year's resolutions, I was thinking about resigning my position as Lead Pastor of Faith Community Church, searching for my replacement, or considering telling the board we needed to shut down. We were really at a dead end.

I was tired. I was broken. I was defeated. I was out of ideas. I was out of creativity. I was burnt, broke, and bitter. In 2015, I lost my only sibling, my brother. In the fall of 2018, I lost my biggest fan, my mother. I was pretty much done. Have you ever been there?

Are you there now?

I want you to know God knows all about it. You are not forgotten, you are loved, and He is with you. Don't give up. Don't lose faith. We serve a God who has never lost a single battle. We serve a God who brings light into our darkest hour. We serve a God who can heal the brokenhearted. We serve a God who brings happiness to the hurting.

We Serve The God Who Brings Happiness To The Hurting

In January of 2019 I received an email from Pastor Jonathan Barker from the Wadsworth Nazarene Church in Wadsworth, Ohio. He invited me to have lunch with him to discuss a great opportunity to reach our communities in Wadsworth and Orrville.

Within a few moments of our meeting, I told him I was looking for a building, and he told me he had a building and within just a few months of our meeting, we began to watch God do the impossible, not just once, but over and over again.

We merged three churches into one church with two separate campuses. We went from about $26,000 in total assets to over $5 million. We went from no acres to over eight acres of land. We went from no building to two buildings with a third building that opened in October 2020 with our third church campus.

Our church in Orrville went from fifty people to over two-hundred people. As I shared earlier, in May of 2019 an anonymous donor gave us $130,000 to jump-start a capital campaign to upgrade our facilities, and most importantly, as I type these words it continues to change daily. Because God continues to grow His church, we've had ninety-six people come to the saving power of Jesus Christ, all in the middle of a global pandemic. So when I say, I believe God can do anything, I truly believe God can do anything.

Every time I walk into our church building for a meeting, for work purposes, or for a service, I am reminded that God can do anything! Every time I look in the undeveloped back field of our property and dream of a family life center, a day care, a Christian academy, or indoor playgrounds for our families to come and hang out in during cold winter days, I am reminded that God can do anything.

The dreams haven't ended; they have just begun. God is not tired. He is not worn-out. There is no shortage on His miracle working power. There are plenty of shortages in our world, but there will never be a shortage on God's resources. God gives because of His grace and we receive whatever He is distributing through our faith. Currently I serve as the Lead Pastor at Now Church. A friend recently said to me, "Only God could take a little scruffy hill-billy baptist boy and make him a Lead Pastor over 3 Nazarene Churches." Exactly! Only God, because He can do anything!

There Is No Shortage On God-Given Resources

Romans 11 says,

Oh, the depth of the riches both of the wisdom and knowledge of God! How unsearchable are His judgments and His ways past finding out!
    "For who has known the mind of the Lord,
     Or who became His counselor?"
    Or who has first given to Him

And it shall be repaid to him?"
For of Him and through Him and to Him
are all things, to whom be the glory forever.
Amen. (Romans 11:33–36)

God makes it clear over and over again, that He is all we need. But before we seek His hand of provision, we must seek His face, and before we seek His face, we must fall at His feet.

Before We Seek His Face, We Must Bow At His Feet

In Jeremiah 33 God says, "Call to Me, and I will answer you, and show you great and mighty things, which you do not know" (Jer. 33:3).
God has given us His menu.
What are you ordering?

God Has Given Us His Menu. What Are You Ordering?

Notice Jeremiah doesn't say, call your buddies; Google search it; or buy another self-help book. He says, "Call to Me!" He has given us the way, and He has given us His Word.

Call to God, and He will answer you. We receive from God through a relationship with Him. We receive through His Word, through the power of His Holy Spirit, through time spent in prayer, through the good news of His gospel, and through all of His creation.

He reaches down, we reach up, and a bond is formed.

And possibly the greatest display of this intimacy between His grace and our faith in all of Scripture is found in Psalm 23. King David gives us this view of God that guides us into the details of the connection between God's grace and our faith found in a relationship that a creature can have with his or her Maker.

Psalm 23:1 says, "The Lord is my shepherd; I shall not want." God is our source for everything. The Lord is our provider.

Verse 2 says, "He makes me to lie down in green pastures; He leads me beside the still waters." God is our source of rest and peace.

Verse 3 says, "He restores my soul." God restores our soul. The Lord is our healer. "He leads me in the paths of righteousness For His name's sake." God is our righteousness. The Lord is our righteousness, not I but Christ.

Verse 4 says, "Yea, though I walk through the valley of the shadow of death, I will fear no evil; for You are with me; Your rod and Your staff, they comfort me." God is the source for our protection. The Lord is with us. He strength assures us with comfort. The Lord is our comforter.

Verse 5 says, "You prepare a table before me in the presence of my enemies; You anoint my head with oil." God is our source of joy and celebration. We only boast in what the Lord has done. The Lord provides us with purpose in service to Him.

Then King David concludes verse 5 with this bold statement: "My cup runs over" (Ps. 23:5).

My cup runs over. Whisper those words right now.

My cup runs over. Our cups are filled with past memories, good and bad. Our cups are filled with laughter and pain. Our cups are filled with future anticipation. With all of this, His goodness and mercy continue to pour into our cups, and our cups overflow.

Do you have a favorite cup? If you come to visit my home, I would ask you if you'd like something to drink, and more than likely I would offer you a cup of coffee because I love coffee.

I love to make coffee for guests who come into our home and we have some pretty awesome cups at our house. We have cups from Starbucks, Disney,

Duck Dynasty. We have a few cups with beautiful art-work on them. We even have some cups purchased at The Dollar Tree. There's a chance I would pour your coffee in any of those cups, because I would be willing to share any of those cups with you. However, there is one cup I can promise you, I wouldn't allow you to us, because it's my cup.

When my son, Hutson, was in second grade during the Santa's Workshop visit at his elemen-tary school, he purchased this cup for me. It's a simple, red, white, and blue ceramic cup that on the outside of the cup says two words in bold letters, *"HERO DAD."*

That's my cup, and you can't drink from it. I think many times we hear great stories of what God has done for others, we see God move in mighty ways in the lives of others, or we read books like this one and think, "Good for them but not me." Or we think, "I want to be blessed like them," and we try to drink from their cups. But that's not how God has it designed for us. King David makes it clear, "My cup runs over." It's my cup. It's my relationship with God and it runs over. It's not half-full or half-empty and it's not filled to the brim of perfection but it is run-ning over. My cup runs over. God never runs out of provisions. We all have more than enough for our every need. If we are connected with Him, He will take care of each and every one of us. We all can say as the Psalmist said: "He is my shepherd. He leads me. He comforts me. He protects me. He provides for me. He fills me. I am fully connected to the God of the universe; I belong to Him."

It's not just "a" cup, it's "my" cup. It's not my "Mommy's" cup, "Daddy's" cup, or "Granny's" cup. It's my cup. It's not a "church" cup, or a "community" cup. It's my cup. Maybe the reason your cup isn't being filled up is because you're trying to drink from someone else's cup.

The most important relationship that you and I should be working on is our relationship with God. This is where real joy comes from. A doubting heart will never be filled with joy. Faith in God fills our hearts with happiness. When the Good Shepherd fills up your cup, He fills it with abundance and out of His abundance flows rivers of joy that will never run dry.

Faith In God Fills Our Hearts with Joy

King David wraps up this famous chapter by saying this:

Surely goodness and mercy shall follow me

All the days of my life;
And I will dwell in the house of the Lord
Forever. (Psalm 23:6)

David was writing this as an old man. He was writing this not as the shepherd boy, or a rock slinging giant slayer, not as a king, but as a man who was nearing the end of his life.

David looked back over his life and in spite of all of his sin, all of his failures, he knew he had been followed by God's mercy, goodness, and unfailing love. Why? Because God gives, He gives His grace over and over again. It will never run out.

As the people of God, we can claim these same assurances by faith:

God's covenant with us is not going to fail.

God's promises can be trusted, no matter what the circumstances may be.

His resources are unlimited, and they will never run out.

The covenant of God, the power of God, the promises of God, these are all spiritual resources we can depend on as we claim our inheritance in Jesus Christ.

When God says, "I can do anything," He says it to you and to me. He says it to all who will believe.

Lord, increase my faith.

Grace reaches down. Faith reaches up. Miracles happen in between.

Appendix:

Introduction:

1. *Pg. 4- Plato, The Republic*

2. *Pg. 4- Towns, Elmer, (1998) What Faith Is All About. Custom Publishing*

3. *Pg. 5- Merriam-Webster Online Dictionary copyright © 2021 by Merriam-Webster, Incorporated*

4. *NKJV All Scripture Scripture taken from the New King James Version®. Copyright © 1982 by Thomas Nelson. Used by permission. All rights reserved.*

Chapter 1 It's a Boy!

1. *NKJV Scriptures NKJV All Scripture Scripture taken from the New King James Version®.*

2. *(Pg 15 Luke 1:37) New Century Version The Holy Bible, New Century Version®. Copyright © 2005 by <u>Thomas Nelson, Inc.</u>*

Chapter 2 Anything?

1. *NKJV Scripture NKJV All Scripture Scripture taken from the New King James Version®. Copyright © 1982 by Thomas Nelson. Used by permission. All rights reserved.*

2. *(Pg.24-25) <u>WhiteHouse.Gov</u> Harrison The Presidents of the United States of America," by Frank Freidel and Hugh Sidey. Copyright 2006 by the White House Historical Association.*

3. *(Pg. 25) <u>wilderness.org</u> How America Started Saving National Forests © 2022 The Wilderness Society. All Rights Reserved.*

Chapter 3 Anything!

1. *NKJV Scriptures NKJV All Scripture Scripture taken from the New King James Version®. Copyright © 1982 by Thomas Nelson. Used by permission. All rights reserved.*

2. Pg. 34 Ed Hindson "Courageous Faith Life Lessons from the Old Testament."

Chapter 4 Consequences Of Unbelief

1. *NKJV Scriptures NKJV All Scripture Scripture taken from the New King James Version®. Copyright © 1982 by Thomas Nelson. Used by permission. All rights reserved.*

Chapter 5 Fear and Unbelief

1. *NKJV Scriptures NKJV All Scripture Scripture taken from the New King James Version®. Copyright © 1982 by Thomas Nelson. Used by permission. All rights reserved.*

2. *pg. 59 Merriam-Webster Online Dictionary copyright © 2021 by Merriam-Webster, Incorporated*

Chapter 6 Fire From A Recliner

1. *NKJV Scriptures NKJV All Scripture Scripture taken from the New King James Version®. Copyright © 1982 by Thomas Nelson. Used by permission. All rights reserved.*

2. Pg. 68 Warren Wiersbe ((*The Wiersbe Study Bible, New King James Version* Copyright 2009, 2018 by Warren W. Wiersbe)

3. Pg. 77 Proverbs 3:5-6 (King James Version)

Chapter 7 Grab the Bags

1. *NKJV Scriptures NKJV All Scripture Scripture taken from the New King James Version®. Copyright © 1982 by Thomas Nelson. Used by permission. All rights reserved.*

2. Pg. 81 Latin, twelfth century; trans, John Mason Neale 1818–1866, 1851) Internet http://www.

hymnsandcarolsofchristmas.com/Hymns_and_Carols/o_come_o_come_emmanuel-1.htm

Chapter 8 Talk to the Hand

1. *NKJV Scriptures NKJV All Scripture Scripture taken from the New King James Version®. Copyright © 1982 by Thomas Nelson. Used by permission. All rights reserved.*

Chapter 9 Two Ears One Mouth

1. *NKJV Scriptures NKJV All Scripture Scripture taken from the New King James Version®. Copyright © 1982 by Thomas Nelson. Used by permission. All rights reserved.*

Chapter 10 It Is What It Is

1. *NKJV Scriptures NKJV All Scripture Scripture taken from the New King James Version®. Copyright © 1982 by Thomas Nelson. Used by permission. All rights reserved.*

2. pg. 118 Abraham Lincoln quote goodreads.com © 2022 Goodreads, Inc. Mobile Version

3. Pg. 118 Dwight Eisenhower quote The Bible Is The Word Of God, March 21, 2022 by Wenda Grabau https://fillmorecountyjournal.com/the-bible-is-the-word-of-god/© 2022 · Website Design and Hosting by SMG Web Design of Preston, MN.

4. Pg. 118 Charles Dickens quote The Bible Is The Word Of God, March 21, 2022 by Wenda Grabau https://fillmorecountyjournal.com/the-bible-is-the-word-of-god/© 2022 · Website Design and Hosting by SMG Web Design of Preston, MN.

5. Pg. 118 Ronald Regan quote goodreads.com © 2022 Goodreads, Inc. Mobile Version

Chapter 11 I Got This

1. *NKJV Scriptures NKJV All Scripture Scripture taken from the New King James Version®. Copyright © 1982 by Thomas Nelson. Used by permission. All rights reserved.*

2. pg. 129 John C. Maxwell quote (BrainyQuote. com) © 2001–2022 BrainyQuote

Chapter 12 No!

1. *NKJV Scriptures NKJV All Scripture Scripture taken from the New King James Version®. Copyright © 1982 by Thomas Nelson. Used by permission. All rights reserved.*

Chapter 13 Pin the Tail on the False Prophet

1. *NKJV Scriptures NKJV All Scripture Scripture taken from the New King James Version®. Copyright © 1982 by Thomas Nelson. Used by permission. All rights reserved.*

2. pg. 149 Bible Stats (https://www.statista.com/statistics/299433/bible-readership-in-the-usa/ Statista Inc. 3 World Trade Center 175 Greenwich Street; 36th Floor New York, NY 10007 United States

Chapter 14 My Cup

1. *NKJV Scriptures NKJV All Scripture Scripture taken from the New King James Version®. Copyright © 1982 by Thomas Nelson. Used by permission. All rights reserved.*

Acknowledgments

I want to praise God for allowing me to share this book with the world. It has been a long process, but worth every minute of it. I truly believe that with God all things are possible. To my wife Angela, I love and appreciate you so much, thanks for being there for me. Thanks for supporting my crazy ideas. To my son Hutson, thanks for being a true gift from the Lord. Your kindness towards others, work ethic, and wisdom is something our world needs a lot more of. I love you. Dad, thank you for providing a christian home environment for me to grow in God's grace in. Norm Pratt, I appreciate you so much. Thank you for allowing me to never give up on my dreams, and always being sensitive to the Holy Spirit as you pour into my life. Derek Temple, you are the most creative and talented person I have ever met. Your attention to detail is something most in our world overlook. Thank you for putting my words into pictures. Now Church, each and every one of you can find yourself in this story. You are an answer to prayer, thank you for laying your personal preferences aside and believing that with God all things are possible. To all my friends and family members, it is my prayer that each of you will be blessed by this book as much as I have been blessed to have you in my life.

About The Author

Pastor Jim Copenhaver was saved and baptized at an early age under the ministry of his lifelong friend and mentor Pastor Dan Wingate of West Hill Baptist Church in Wooster, Ohio. As a teenager he felt the call of God upon his life to dedicate his life to the ministry of the gospel of Jesus Christ. Jim preached his first sermon at the age of sixteen and has never looked backed.

In 2006, Jim started singing with his mother and brother in a family trio. They traveled and sang together for about seven years. During that time The Copenhavers teamed up with an evangelistic team out of Lynchburg, Virginia, with the dynamic preaching of Dr. Norm Pratt and Dr. Dan DeHass. During that time, Jim started traveling with the award-winning GloryWay Quartet out of Mansfield, Ohio. After traveling with them for about three years, Jim felt a great desire, call, and burden for the local church. He knew that God was calling him to start a church, so by faith he started Faith Community Church in the Kingsway Christian School gymnasium.

Pastor Jim and his friend Pastor Josh Evans teamed up to launch a Liberty Church Network local center in Orrville, Ohio, which was a first for the entire state. Through the local center, pastors come together to connect, care, communicate, and equip one another to make disciples of Jesus Christ in their local assemblies. In its short existence, God has done many great things through the LCN local center.

In 2019, Jim teamed up with Pastor Jonathan Barker from the First Church of The Nazarene in Wadsworth. Together they merged three churches, two different denominations, into one church at two locations. They have developed Now Church, which is a thriving multi-site church focused on making disciples of Jesus Christ. They plan to launch more churches as they grow and see needs in surrounding communities.

Pastor Jim has over twenty years of ministry experience and he's just as excited about what God has in store for the future. His passion to share the gospel of Jesus Christ and equip others to do so, is the driving force behind his ministry. Jim received his Biblical Studies certificate from Liberty University and is also the recipient of an honorary Doctorate of Divinity. He and his wife Angela, and their son, Hutson, and live in Wooster, Ohio.